Creation Station

Learning Center Projects for Art

Written by **Jean Warren** and **Gayle Bittinger**
Illustrated by **Marilynn Barr**

Totline® **Publications**
A Division of Frank Schaffer Publications, Inc.
Torrance, California

Managing Editor: Kathleen Cubley

Editors: Carol Gnojewski, Susan Hodges, Elizabeth McKinnon

Copyeditor: Kris Fulsaas

Proofreader: Miriam Bulmer

Editorial Assistant: Durby Peterson

Graphic Designer/Layout Artist: Sarah Ness/Gordon Frasier

Graphic Design (Cover): Brenda Mann Harrison

Production Manager: Melody Olney

ISBN: 1-57029-161-6

Library of Congress Catalog Number 97-62225
Printed in the United States of America
Published by Totline® Publications
Editorial Office: P.O. Box 2250
     Everett, WA 98203
Business Office: 23740 Hawthorne Blvd.
     Torrance, CA 90505

20 19 18 17 16 15 14 13 12 11 10 9 8 7 6 5 4 3 2

Introduction

Working at stations is a great way to introduce your children to new concepts, reinforce concepts already learned, practice skills, and have fun while learning. Station work also gives them opportunities to work independently, remember and follow directions, and complete projects—important skills for future learning.

The stations in this book, *Creation Station,* are focused on open-ended, child-created art projects. Arranged alphabetically, there are 38 different ideas for making a variety of projects. Simply choose a project that fits the materials you have on hand or the day's lessons, and you are on your way.

Each station activity includes a reproducible "project worksheet" that shows, in words and pictures, the steps the children must follow to make their projects. Each activity also has objectives identifying the skills used while making the project, a list of materials needed, and directions for setting up the station.

Also included are ideas for introducing the project at group time, detailed instructions for making the project, and a teacher-directed follow-up. There are additional reproducible worksheets that extend the topic into additional curriculum areas. These optional worksheets are designed to be worked on in class, as time allows, or at home.

The activities have been written as if one child at a time were working in a station. For more children, simply adjust the materials as needed.

With this book's easy-to-set-up stations and unique reproducible pages, you and your children will enjoy creating all year long as you use activities from *Creation Station.*

Contents

Apple Pie

Objectives

Practice cutting, tearing, and gluing skills.

Materials Needed

❑ plate
❑ cardboard
❑ pen
❑ scissors
❑ construction paper
❑ ground cinnamon
❑ shaker
❑ pencil
❑ glue

Setting Up the Station

• Place a large plate on a sheet of cardboard. Trace around the plate and cut out the circle to make a "pie" pattern.
• Collect brown and red construction paper.
• Put ground cinnamon into a shaker.
• Set out the cardboard circle, construction paper, shaker of cinnamon, a pencil, scissors, and glue.

Introducing the Project

Talk about pies. What makes a pie? Who has eaten a piece of pie? Let your children tell you about all the different pies they have seen and tasted. Which ones were their favorites? Tell them they will be making their own paper Apple Pies, then explain the following project steps.

The Project

1. Place the cardboard circle pattern on a sheet of brown construction paper and trace around it.
2. Cut out the circle shape to make the base of your "pie" and write your name on the back.
3. Tear the red construction paper into apple "slices" and glue them to the pie.
4. Sprinkle a little cinnamon on the pie.

Follow-Up

Serve your children pie for snack. Bring in already baked pies or prepare Biscuit Pies (recipe follows). If you wish, copy the additional worksheets on pages 8 and 9 for the children to complete in class or at home.

Biscuit Pies—Flatten refrigerator biscuits. Add a spoonful of jam to the center of each one. Fold over and seal. Bake at 450°F for 10–12 minutes or until lightly browned.

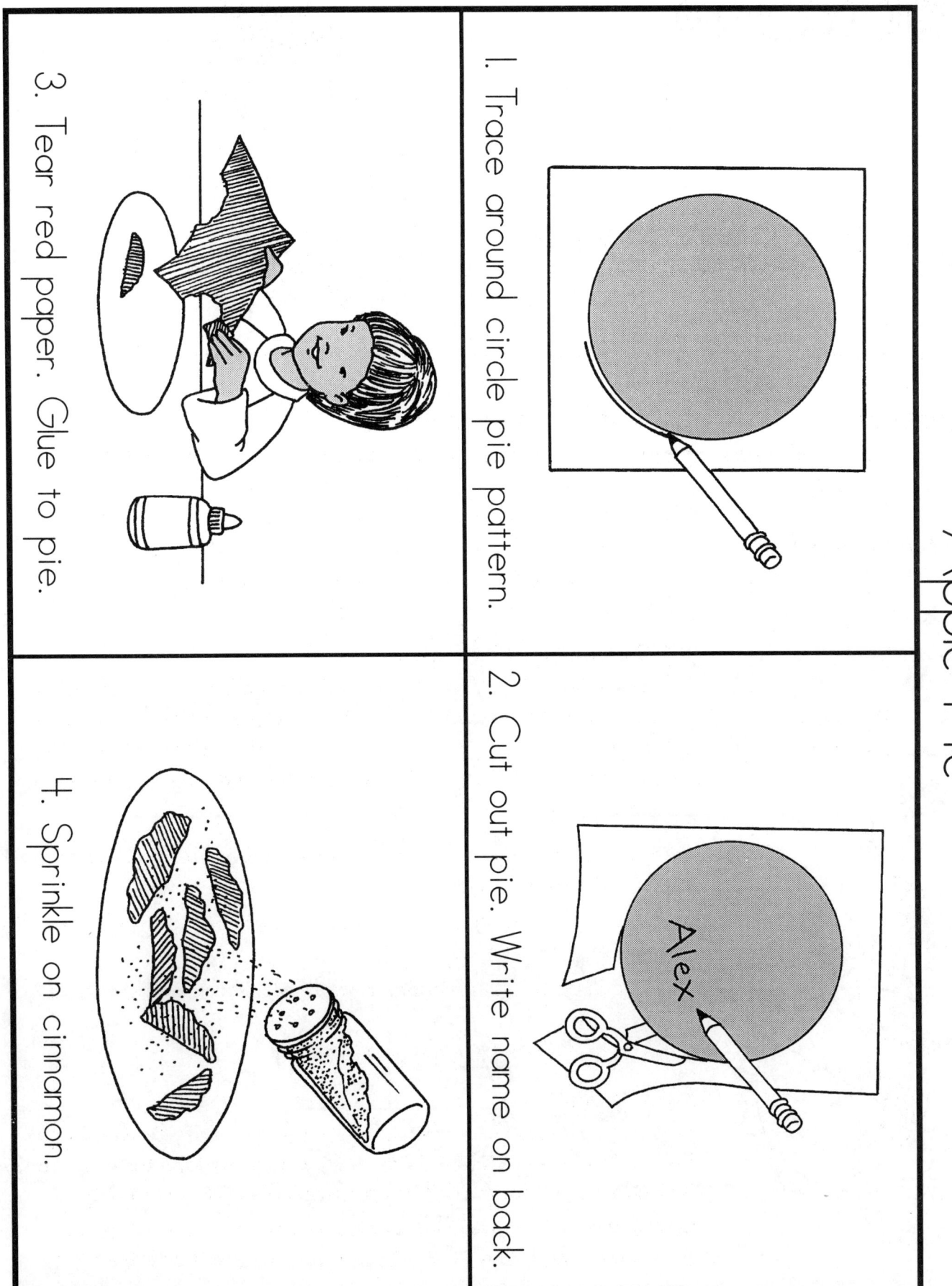

3. Tear red paper. Glue to pie.

1. Trace around circle pie pattern.

4. Sprinkle on cinnamon.

2. Cut out pie. Write name on back.

Apple Pie

Name_____

For each pie, count how many slices have been cut and write that number on the line.

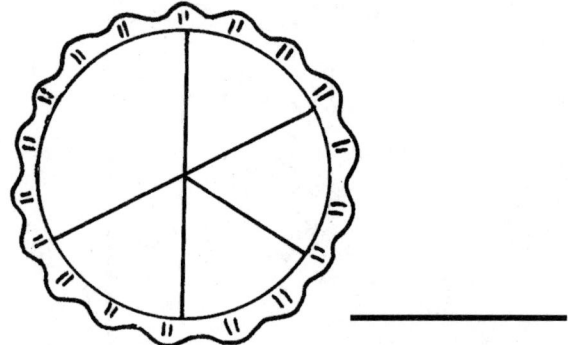 _____

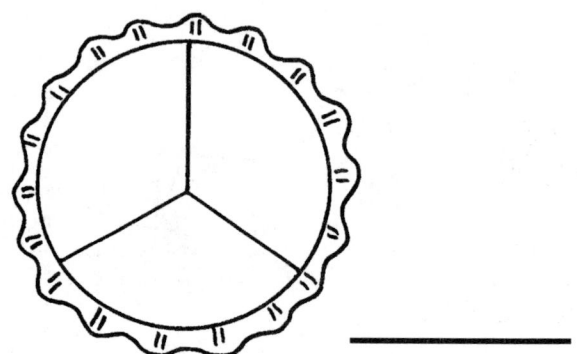 _____

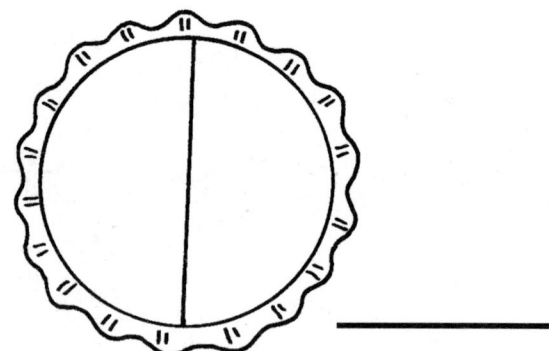 _____

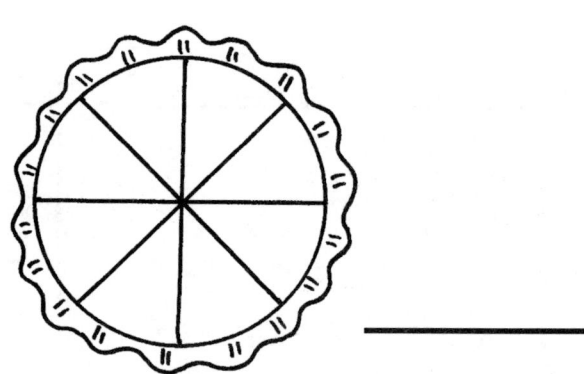 _____

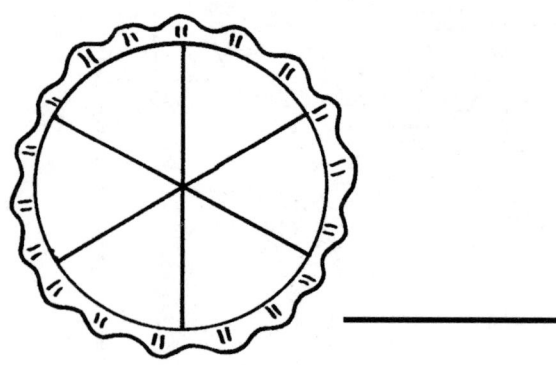 _____

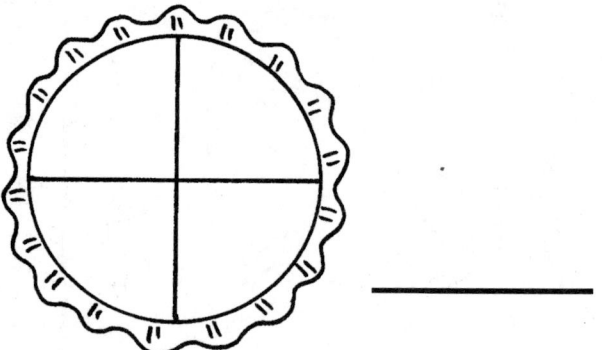 _____

Name_____

Find the items that belong in a pie. Draw a line from each of them to the pie.

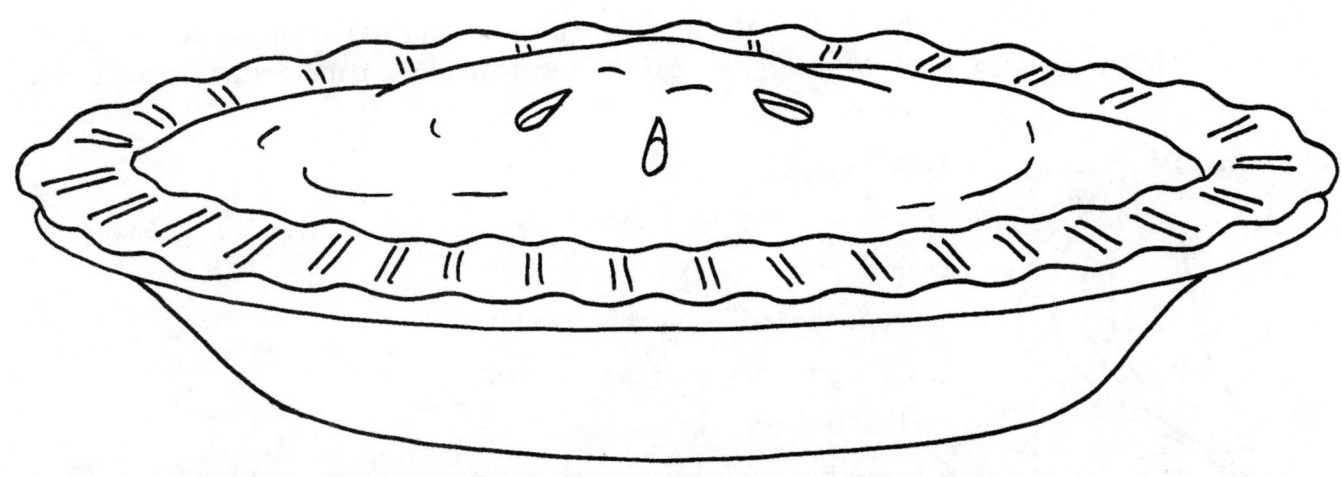

  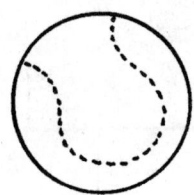

Apple Pie • Creation Station   **9**

Bird of Paradise

Objectives
Use imagination and creativity.

Materials Needed
❑ books with pictures of tropical birds
❑ construction paper
❑ ruler
❑ scissors
❑ stapler
❑ pencil
❑ project worksheets

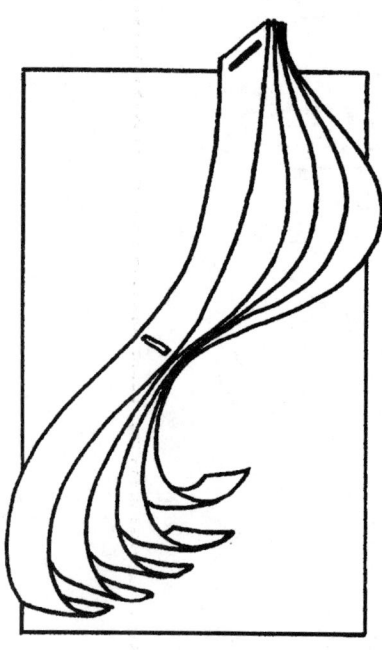

Setting Up the Station
• Set out books with pictures of tropical birds.
• Cut a variety of colors of construction paper into 1-by-12-inch strips.
• Set out the paper strips, a stapler, and a pencil.
• Follow the project directions to make one of the birds.
• Copy and display the project worksheets on pages 11 and 12.

Introducing the Project
Show your children pictures of tropical birds. Have them notice the bright colors and long feathers many of the birds have. What color of bird do they like the best? Show them the bird you made from paper strips. Explain the following project steps to the children, demonstrating how you rolled, curled, and stapled the paper strips together to make the bird.

The Project
1. Choose five of the paper strips.
2. Stack them together in a pile.
3. Staple the strips together at one end.
4. Write your name on the top strip.
5. Hold the top strip straight.
6. Keep the four bottom strips together and make a loop.
7. Staple the bottom strips to the middle of the top strip.
8. Curl the ends of the bottom loops around the pencil to make tail feathers.

Follow-Up
Have the children show you their birds. Help them make any adjustments needed. (Hint: If working with five strips is too hard, let the children make birds with just two or three strips.) Hang the completed birds around the room. If you wish, copy the additional worksheet on page 13 for the children to complete in class or at home.

Bird of Paradise

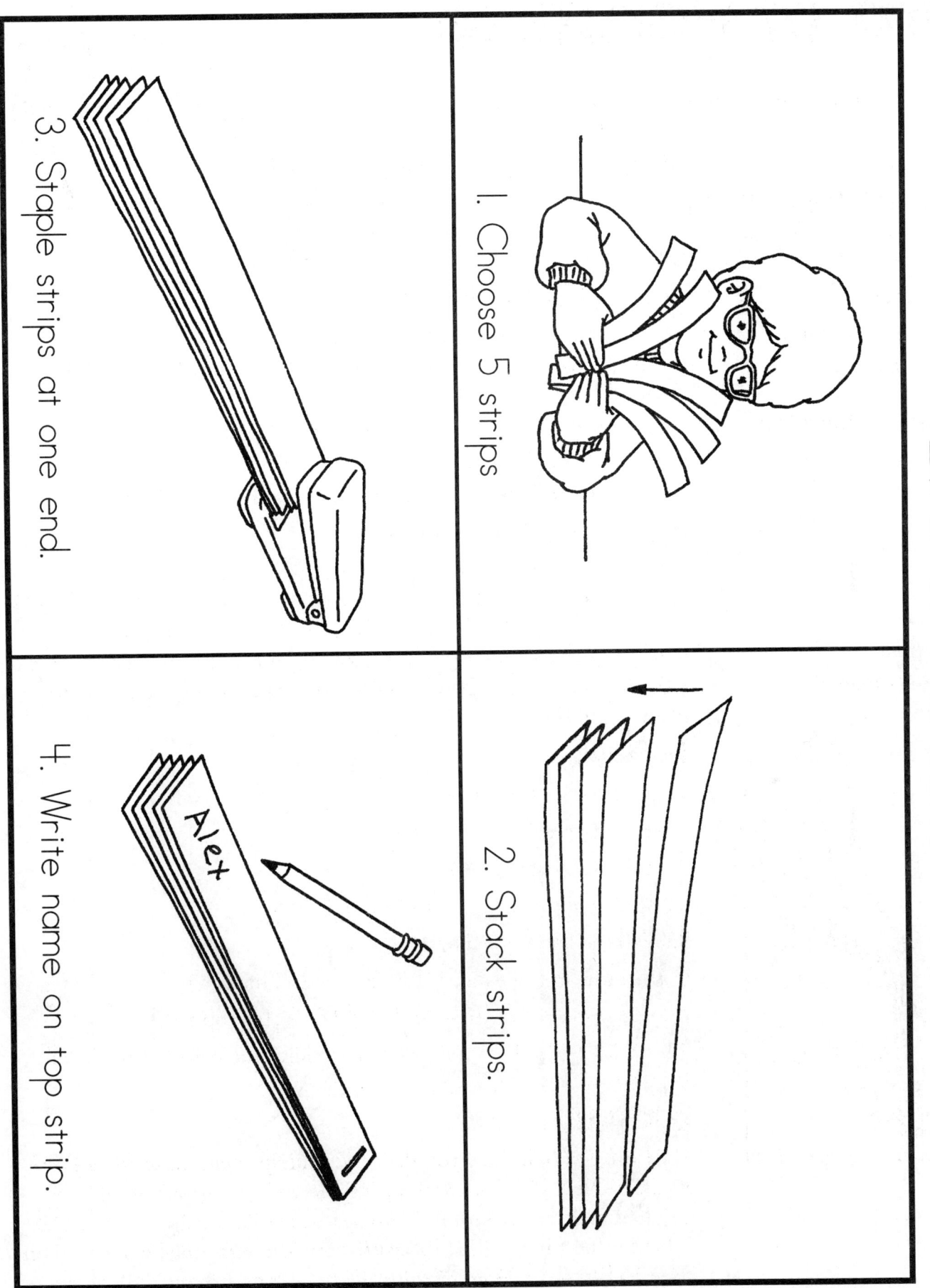

1. Choose 5 strips

2. Stack strips.

3. Staple strips at one end.

4. Write name on top strip.

Alex

Bird of Paradise

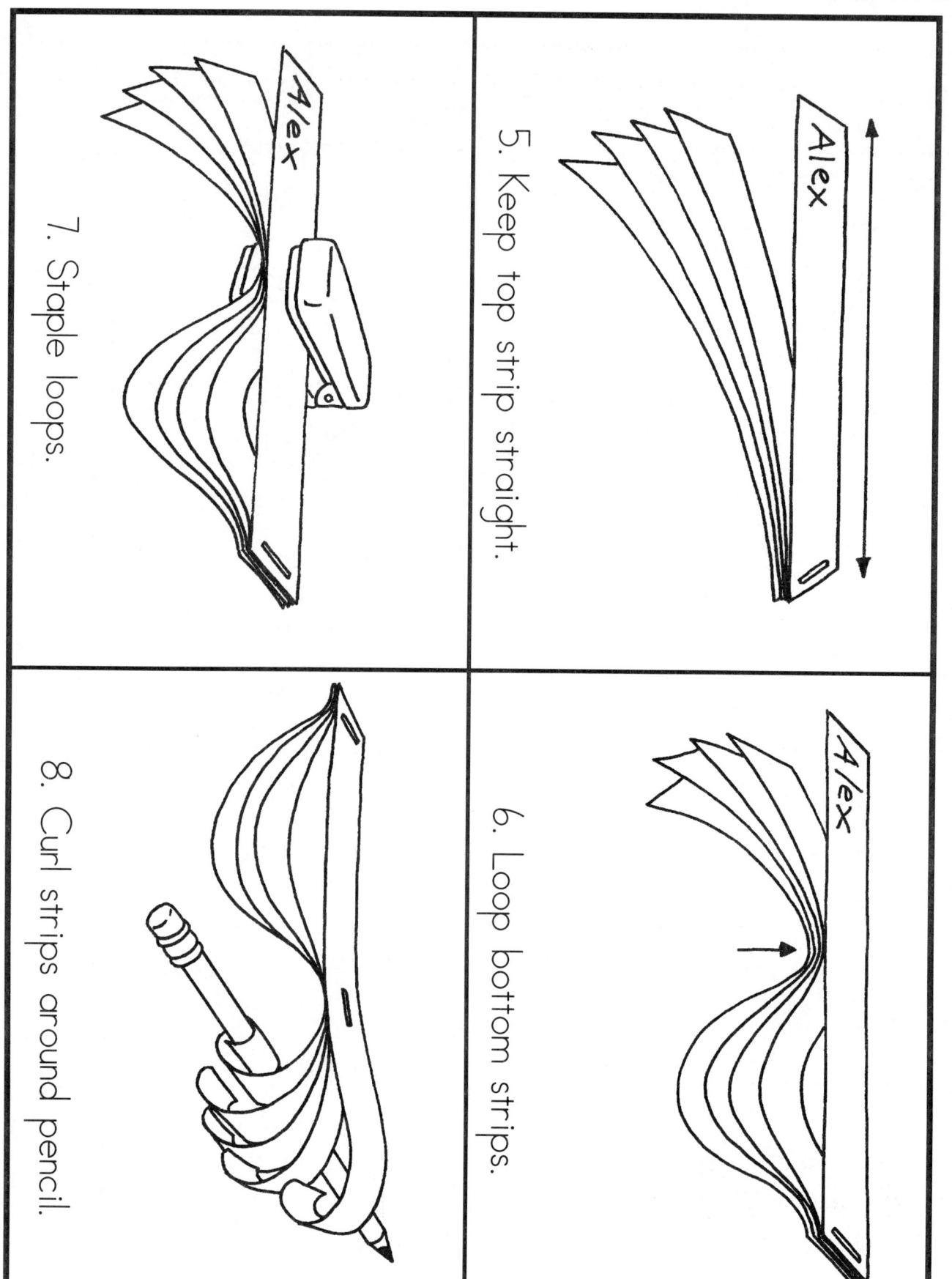

5. Keep top strip straight.

6. Loop bottom strips.

7. Staple loops.

8. Curl strips around pencil.

Name_____

Draw lines to connect the birds that match.

Bird's Nest

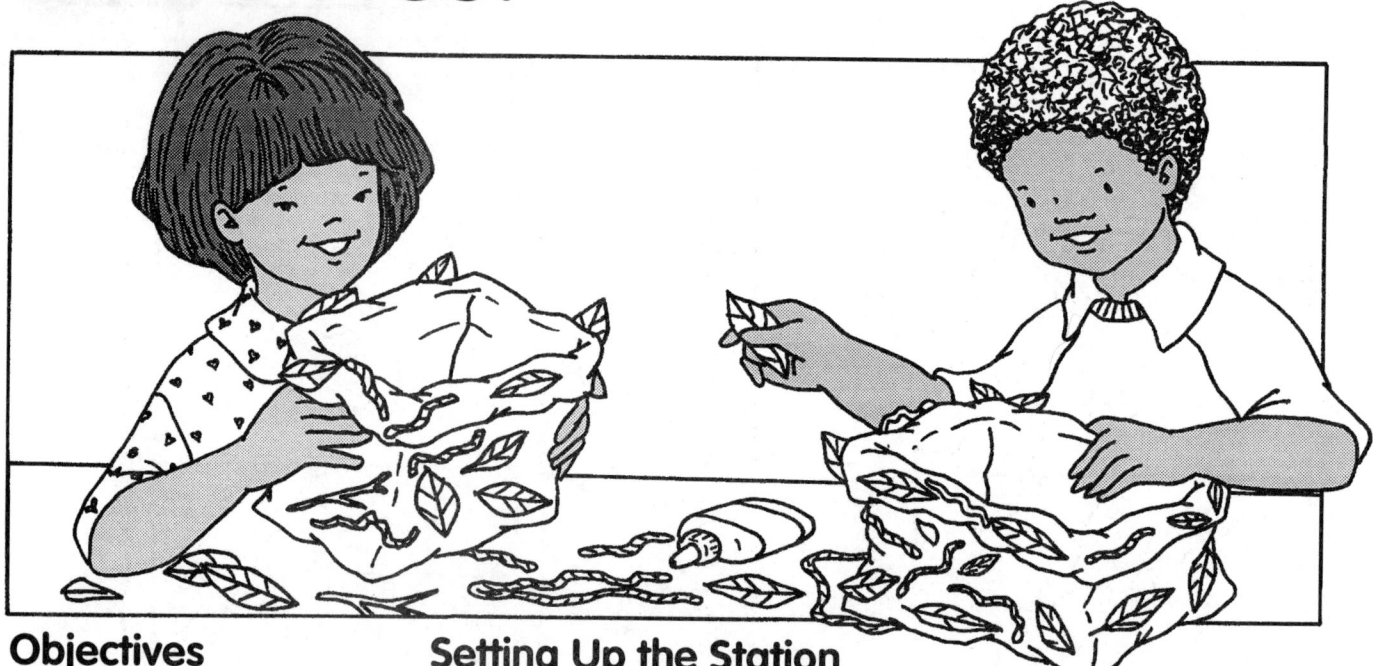

Objectives

Practice gluing skills.

Materials Needed

- ❏ pictures of birds' nests
- ❏ real bird's nest, if possible
- ❏ book about birds' nests
- ❏ nest-building materials
- ❏ paper lunch sacks
- ❏ pencil
- ❏ glue
- ❏ project worksheet

Setting Up the Station

- Set out pictures of birds' nests and, if you have one, a real bird's nest.
- Find a book about birds building nests to show the children.
- Collect nest-building materials such as yarn and straw pieces, lint, feathers, and dried grass.
- Set out the nest-building materials, paper lunch sacks, a pencil, and glue.
- Copy and display the project worksheet on page 15.

Introducing the Project

Show your children the bird's nest or the pictures of birds' nests. Read a book about a bird building a nest. Discuss the materials that birds use to make their nests. Why do they use those materials? Explain the following project steps to the children and let them make their own birds' nests.

The Project

1. Select one of the paper sacks and write your name on the bottom of it.

2. Open up the sack.

3. Roll down the sides of the sack.

4. Glue the nest building materials on the inside and outside of the sack.

Follow-Up

Look at the children's nests. Let them tell you about what materials they used to build their nests. Go on a walk to look for birds' nests in trees and bushes. If you wish, copy the additional worksheets on pages 16 and 17 for the children to complete in class or at home.

Bird's Nest

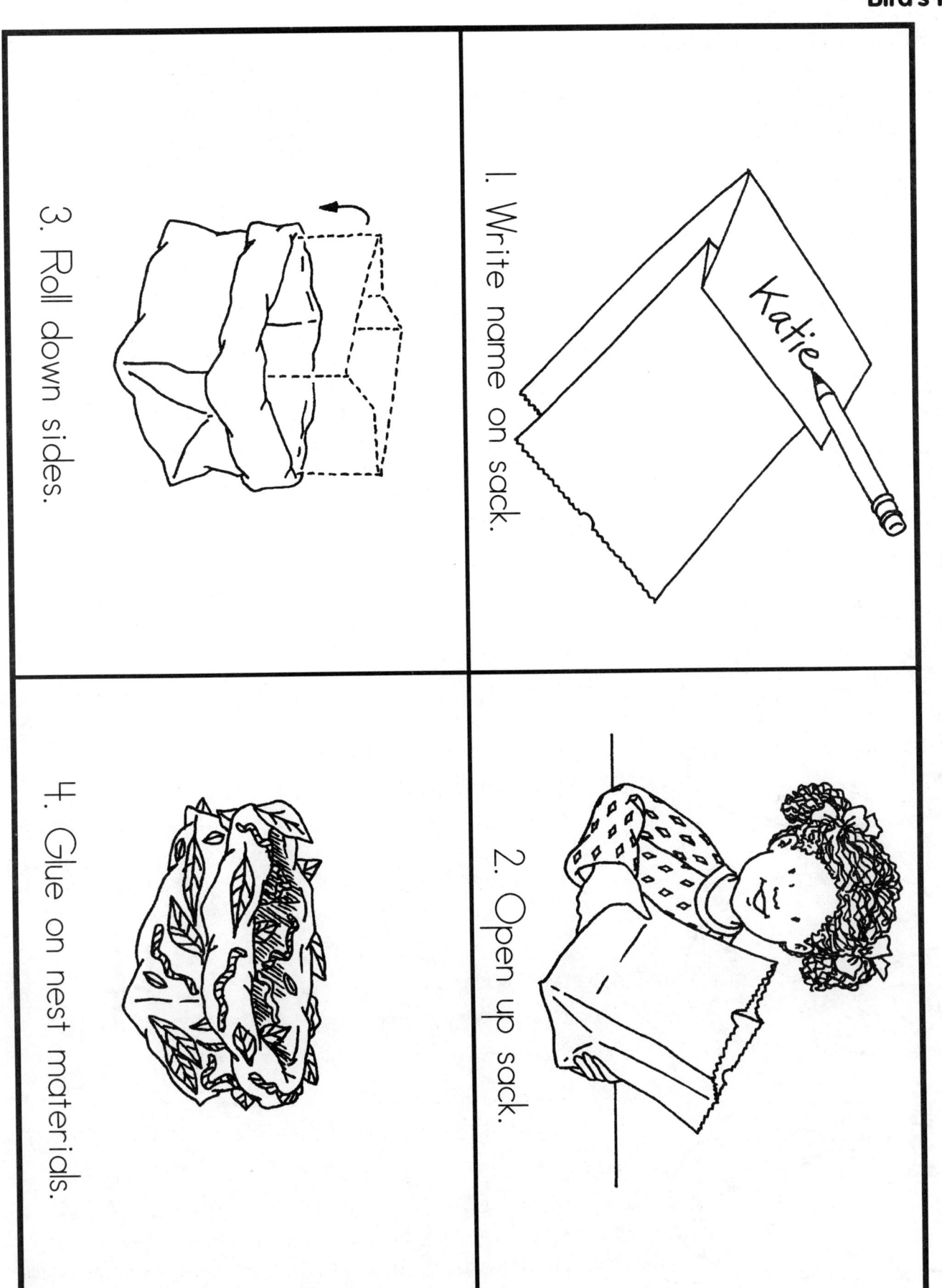

1. Write name on sack.

2. Open up sack.

3. Roll down sides.

4. Glue on nest materials.

Name_____

Count the eggs in each nest and
draw a line to the matching number.

3

7

0

4

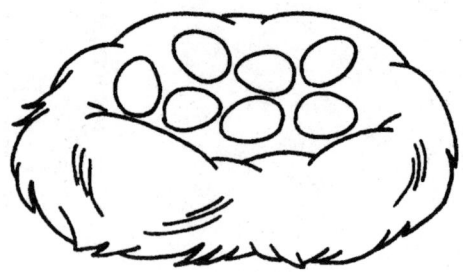

2

Name_____

Help the bird find its nest.

Blot Picture

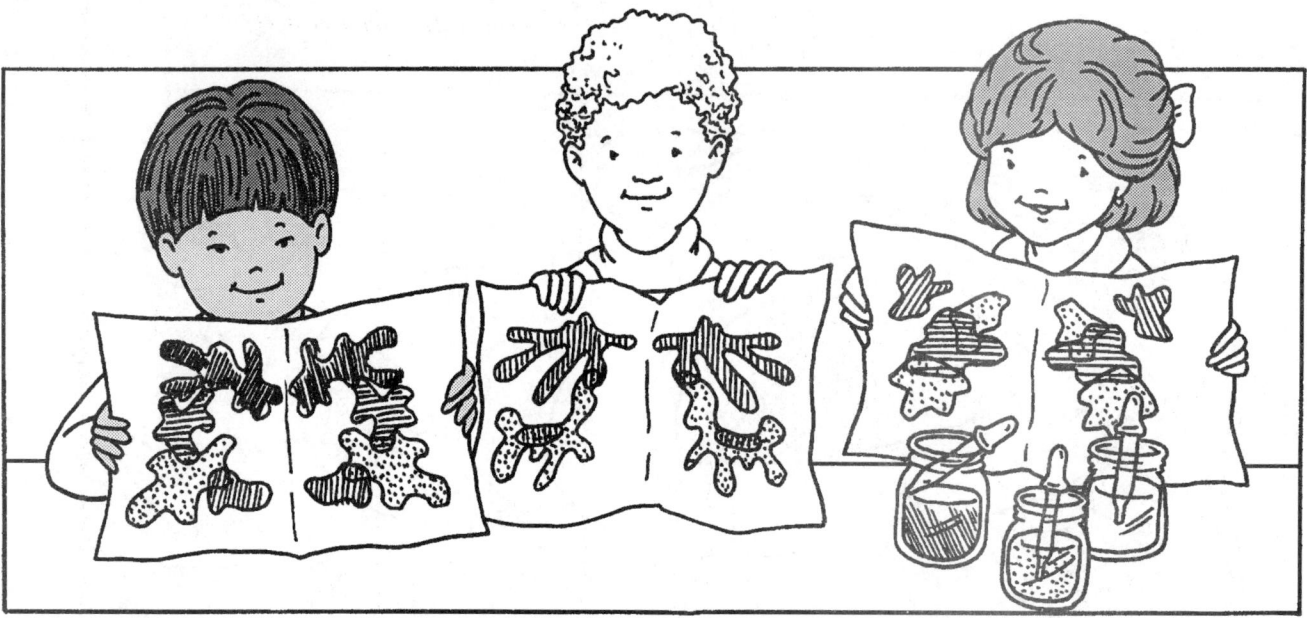

Objectives

Learn about mixing colors and practice small-motor skills.

Materials Needed

❏ tempera paint
❏ baby food jars
❏ water
❏ eyedroppers
❏ white paper
❏ pencil
❏ project worksheet
❏ food coloring
❏ clear glasses
❏ water

Setting Up the Station

- Put red tempera paint in a baby food jar, blue in a second baby food jar, and yellow in a third. Thin each jar of paint with a little water. Place an eyedropper in each jar.
- Set out the jars of paint, white paper, and a pencil.
- Copy and display the project worksheet on page 19.

Introducing the Project

Talk about color mixing with your children. Ask them to tell you what color they get when they mix red and yellow. How about blue and red? Yellow and blue? Drop food coloring into clear glasses of water to demonstrate the new colors that result from the mixing. Explain to the children the following project steps for mixing colors in a new way.

The Project

1. Fold a sheet of paper and write your name on it.

2. Unfold the paper and carefully squeeze out drops of each color of paint on one half.

3. Fold on the crease and gently rub your hand across it.

4. Unfold to reveal the color-mixed design.

Follow-Up

Display the children's colorful pictures. Have them notice all the different colors they made from just red, yellow, and blue. If you wish, copy the additional worksheets on pages 20 and 21 for the children to complete in class or at home.

Blot Picture

1. Fold paper and write name.

Joshua

2. Unfold and squeeze on paint.

3. Fold and rub.

4. Unfold.

Name_____

Color the paint blobs. Finish each color equation.

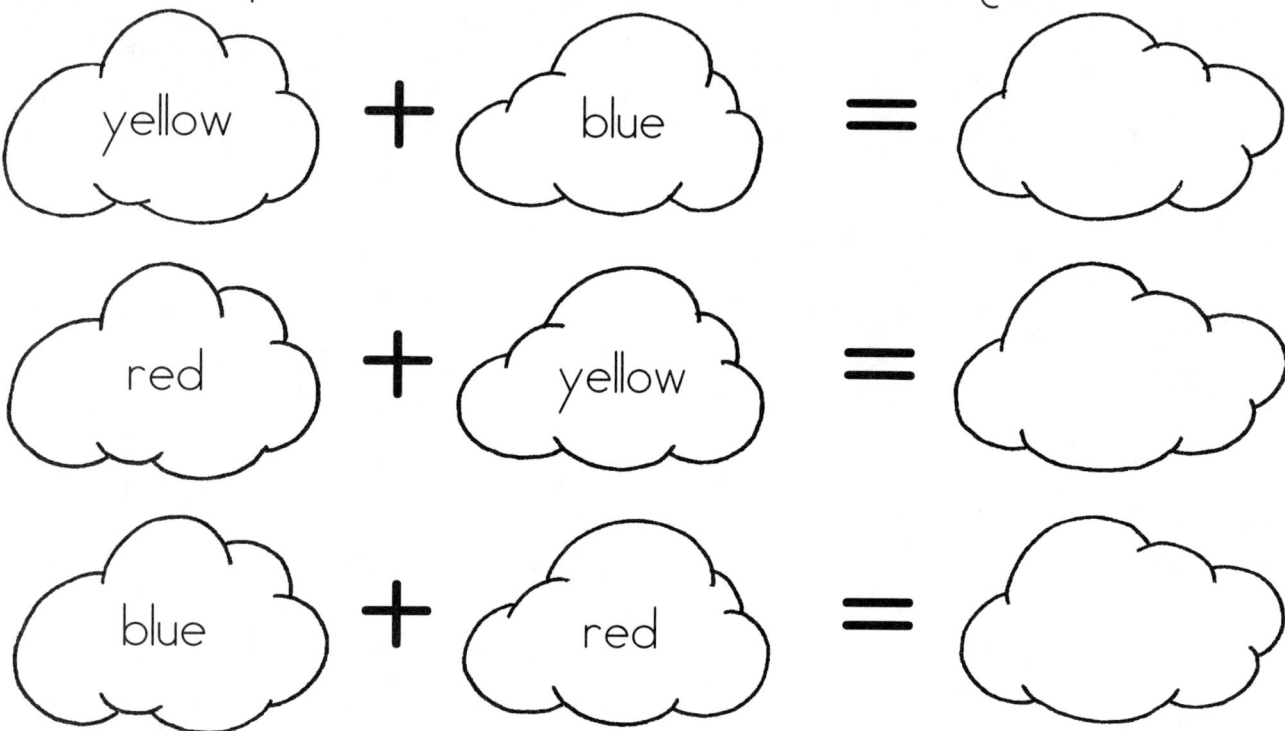

Make up your own color mixing equations.

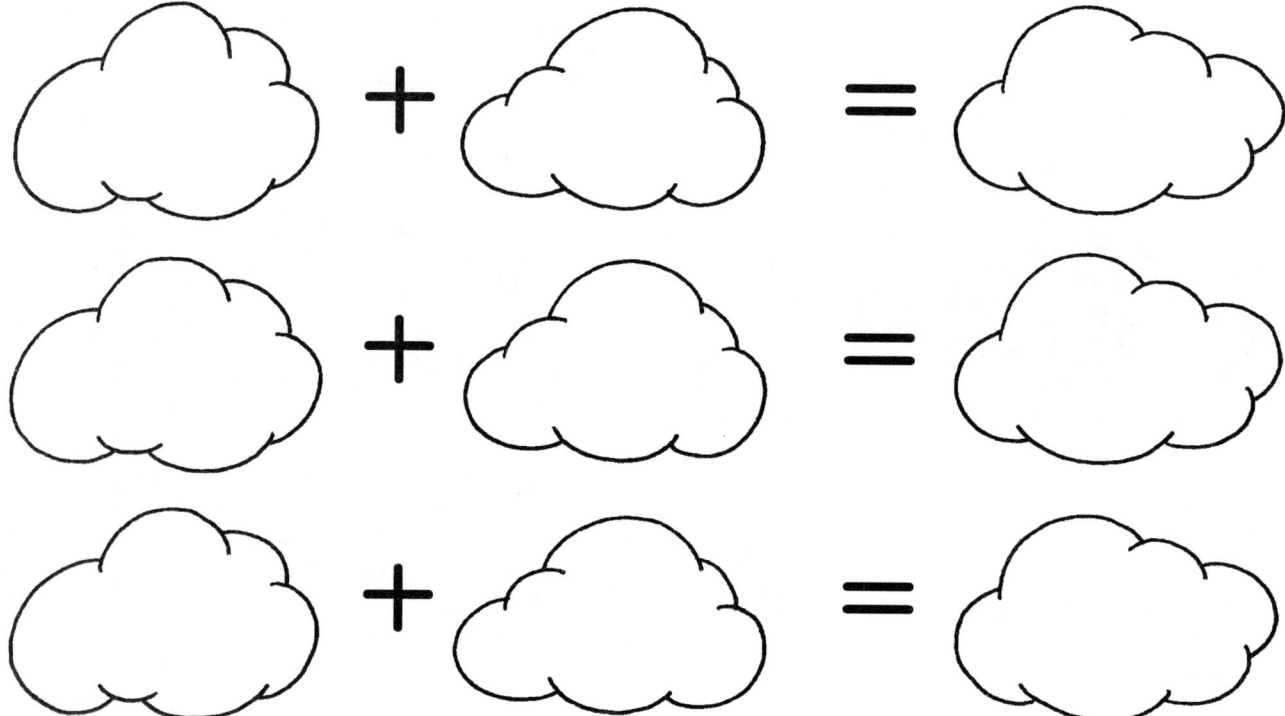

Name_____

Color each part of the rainbow a different color.

Build a Structure

Objectives

Develop creativity, problem-solving, and small-motor skills.

Materials Needed

❑ pictures of buildings
❑ paper plates
❑ pencil
❑ modeling dough
❑ toothpicks
❑ project worksheet

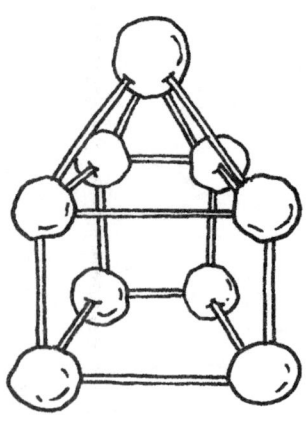

Setting Up the Station

- Hang up pictures of buildings, especially ones under construction.
- Set out paper plates, a pencil, modeling dough, and toothpicks.
- Copy and display the project worksheet on page 23.

Introducing the Project

Talk about building construction with your children. Show them a picture of a building being built. What is happening in the picture? What shapes do they see? How do they think buildings are built? Explain to the children the following project steps and let them experiment with making their own buildings.

The Project

1. Select a paper plate and write your name on it.
2. Roll modeling dough into small balls and place them on the paper plate.
3. Use the dough balls and toothpicks to make the base of the building.
4. Add more toothpicks and dough balls to make the building as tall as you would like.

Follow-Up

Display the children's buildings. Talk about how they are similar and how they are different. If you wish, copy the additional worksheets on pages 24 and 25 for the children to complete in class or at home.

Build a Structure

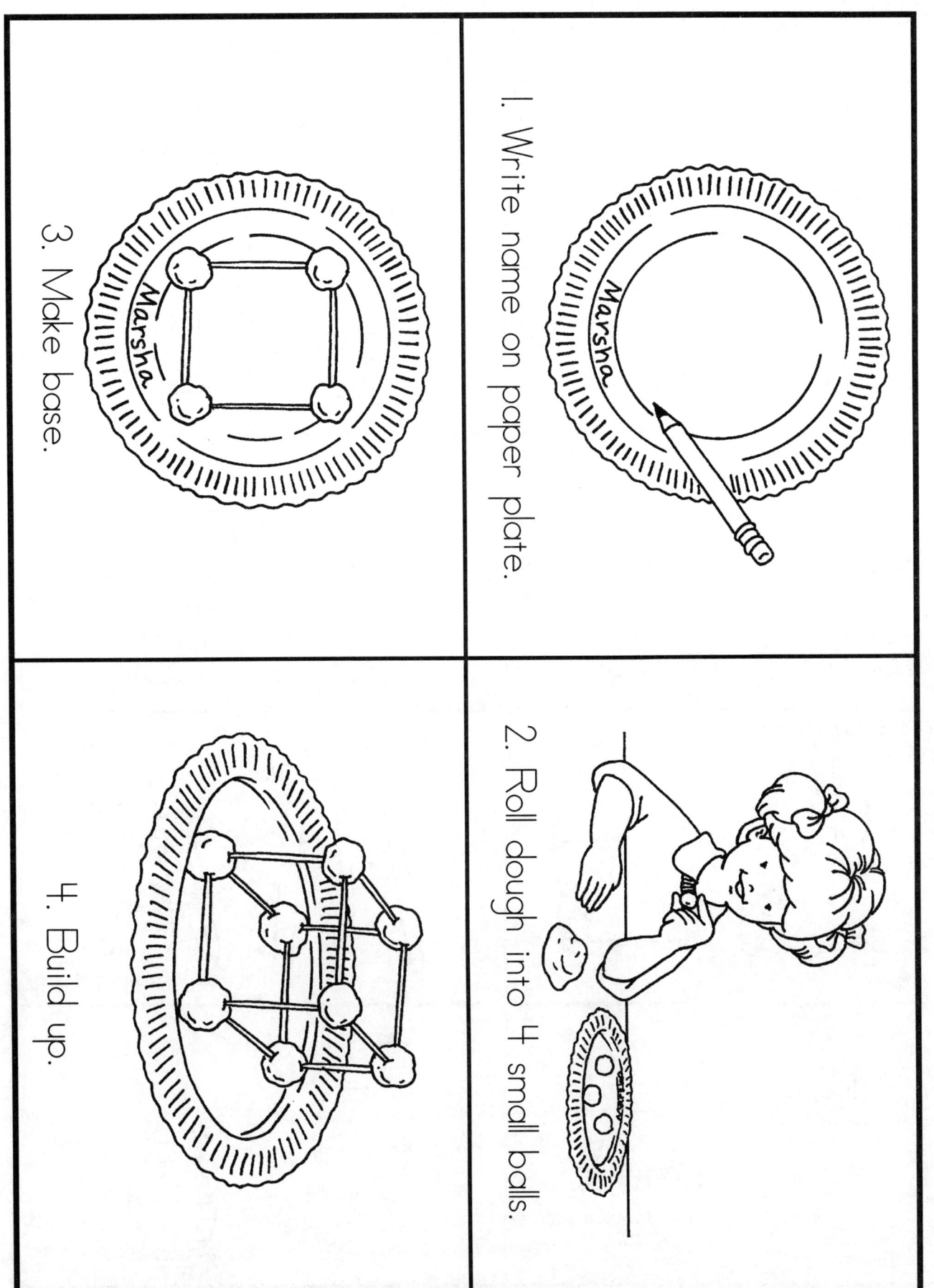

1. Write name on paper plate.

2. Roll dough into 4 small balls.

3. Make base.

4. Build up.

Name_____

For each box, circle the tallest one.

Name_____

Connect the dots to see what the workers are building.

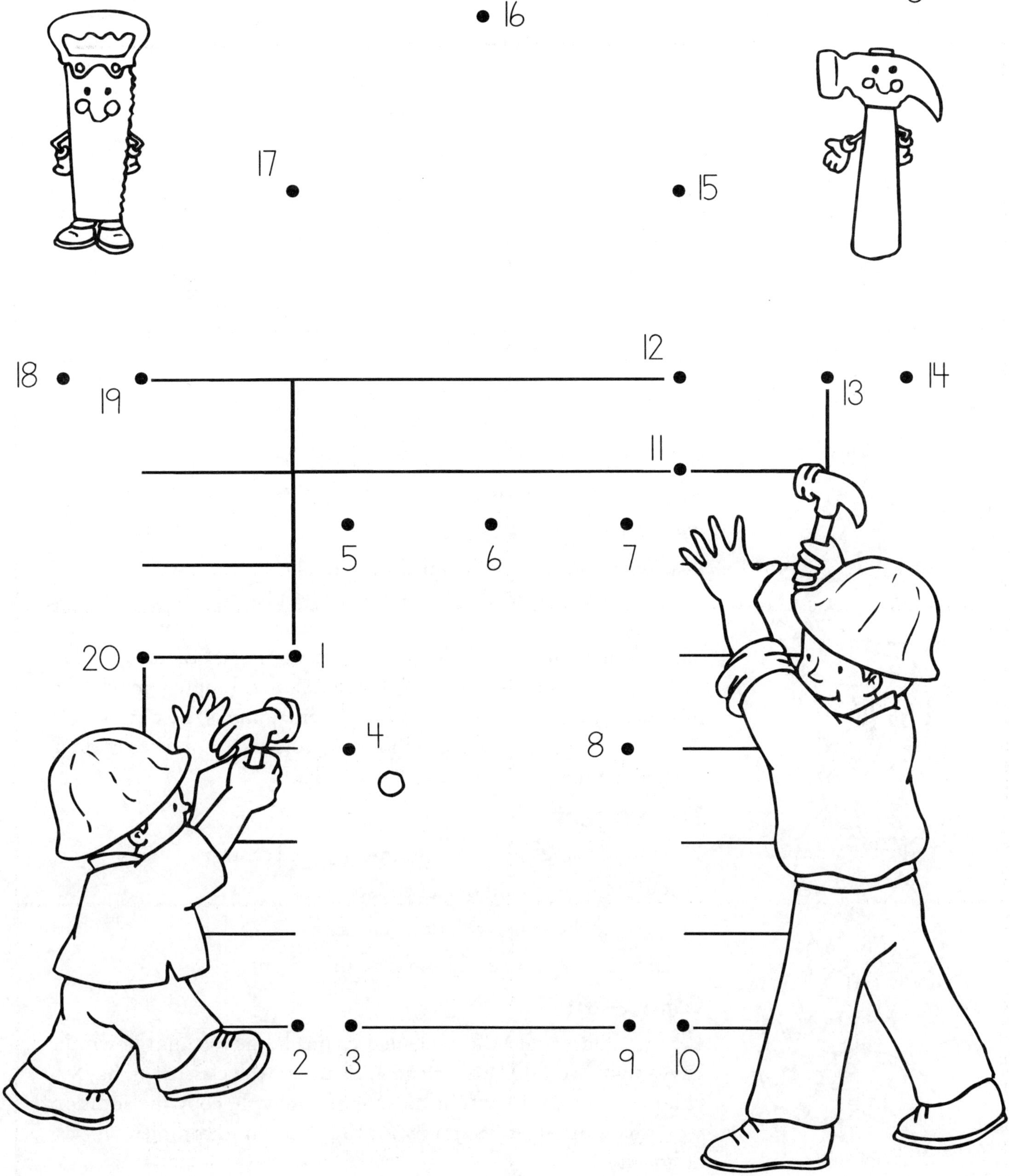

• 16

17 •

• 15

12

18 •   19 •

• 13   • 14

11

5   6   7

20 •   • 1

• 4

8 •

○

2   3   9   10

Calendar Chain

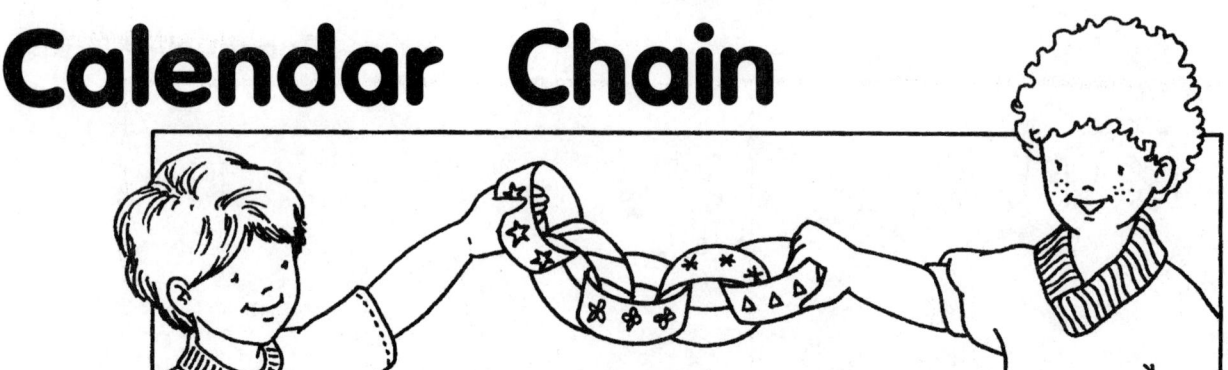

Objectives

Develop creativity and problem-solving skills.

Materials Needed

❑ calendar
❑ holiday decorations
❑ project worksheet
❑ pen
❑ construction paper
❑ scissors
❑ pencil
❑ crayons
❑ tape

Setting Up the Station

- Hang up a calendar, showing the current month.
- Select a holiday that is 10 to 20 days away, such as Valentine's Day. Put up some decorations for that holiday.
- Make a copy of the project worksheet on page 27.
- Count the days left until the holiday you've selected. Write that number on the blank on the worksheet copy. Display this copy in the station.
- Cut construction paper into 1-by-6-inch strips. You will need 10 to 20 strips per child, depending on how far away the holiday is.
- Set out the paper strips, a pencil, crayons, and tape.
- Make a sample Calendar Chain to show the children.

Introducing the Project

Discuss special days with your children. Show them how those days are marked on a calendar. Point out the holiday that will be arriving soon. Let the children help you count the days until that holiday. Show them your Calendar Chain. Tell them that a Calendar Chain can help count down the days before a holiday. Simply remove one link each day, and the number of links remaining is the number of days left to wait. Explain the following project steps to the children so they can make their own Calendar Chains.

The Project

1. Count out the appropriate number of paper strips.
2. Write your name on one of the strips.
3. Decorate the strips with crayon designs.
4. Loop the strips together and tape them in place.

Follow-Up

Let the children take their calendar chains home to count down the days. If you would like a Calendar Chain for the classroom, have the children work together to make one. If you wish, copy the additional worksheets on pages 28 and 29 for the children to complete in class or at home.

Calendar Chain

1. Count out _____ paper strips.

2. Write name on one strip.

Matthew

3. Decorate strips.

4. Loop and tape.

Name_____

Count the loops in each chain. Write the number in the box.

Name_____

Look at each row of numbers.
Write in the missing number.

2	3	___	5	6
1	___	3	4	5
7	8	9	___	11
___	5	6	7	8
8	9	___	11	12
3	4	5	___	7

Circle Picture

Objectives

Practice cutting and gluing skills and develop imagination and creativity.

Materials Needed

❑ circle pictures
❑ circle paper shapes
❑ construction paper
❑ pencil
❑ scissors
❑ glue
❑ project worksheet

Setting Up the Station

• Find pictures of familiar objects that have a circular shape, such as wheels on a car or porthole windows in a ship. Hang them up in the station.

• Collect a variety of sizes of paper circles. These can be purchased at school supply stores or you can cut your own.

• Set out the circle shapes, construction paper, a pencil, scissors, and glue.

• Copy and display the project worksheet on page 31.

Introducing the Project

Show the circle pictures to your children. Let them count all of the circles they can see. Talk about half circles and quarter circles. Have them watch as you cut a circle in half and then in half again. Explain the following project steps to the children.

The Project

1. Select a sheet of construction paper and write your name on the back.

2. Choose the circle shapes you want to work with. Cut some of the circle shapes into half circles or quarter circles.

3. Arrange the circle, half circle, and quarter circle shapes on the construction paper to make your picture.

4. Glue the circles in place.

Follow-Up

Display the children's circle pictures. Let them count how many circles, half circles, and quarter circles were used in their pictures. If you wish, copy the additional worksheets on pages 32 and 33 for the children to complete in class or at home.

1. Write name on paper.

2. Pick circles. Cut some.

3. Arrange circles.

4. Glue in place.

Circle Picture

Name_____

Trace the balloons and color.

Name_____

Color only the circles.

Cotton Ball Art

Objectives

Develop creativity and problem-solving skills.

Materials Needed

❑ glue
❑ bowl
❑ cotton balls
❑ construction paper
❑ pencil
❑ crayons
❑ project worksheet

Setting Up the Station

• Put a small amount of glue into a bowl.
• Set out the bowl of glue, cotton balls, construction paper, a pencil, and crayons.
• Copy and display the project worksheet on page 35.

Introducing the Project

Hold ten cotton balls in your hand. Have your children guess how many there are. Let them count the cotton balls with you. Tell them that they will each be using ten cotton balls to create their own special art project. Then explain the following project steps to them.

The Project

1. Select a sheet of construction paper and write your name on the back of it.
2. Count out ten cotton balls to use in your picture.
3. Dip the cotton balls in the glue and then place them on your paper.
4. Add details with crayons.

Follow-Up

Hang up the children's Cotton Ball Art. How many different kinds of designs did the children make? Were any of the designs the same? If you wish, copy the additional worksheets on pages 36 and 37 for the children to complete in class or at home.

Cotton Ball Art

1. Write name on paper.

Christopher

2. Take 10 cotton balls.

3. Dip in glue and put on paper.

4. Add details.

Name_____

Add up each set of cotton balls. Draw a line to the answer.

 **+** 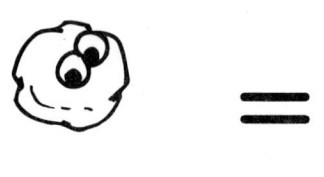 **=**

 **+**  **=**

 **+**  **=**

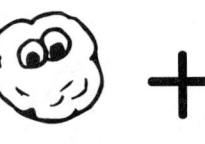 **+**  **=**

 **+** **=**

Name_____

For each box, draw the shapes needed to make 10.

Crayon Resist

Objectives

Develop creativity and small-motor skills.

Materials Needed

❏ tempera paint
❏ water
❏ jars
❏ paintbrushes
❏ apron
❏ construction paper
❏ pencil
❏ crayons
❏ project worksheet

Setting Up the Station

• Make a paint wash by combining one part tempera paint with one part water in a jar. Make several different colors of paint wash.

• Set out the jars of paint wash, paintbrushes, an apron, construction paper, a pencil, and crayons.

• Copy and display the project worksheet on page 39.

Introducing the Project

Talk with your children about shades of colors. Have them look around the room for examples of light and dark colors. Brush a little regular tempera paint on a sheet of white paper, then brush a little of the paint wash next to it. Have the children point to the paint that is a lighter color and the paint that is a darker shade. Explain the following project steps to the children. Ask them to look for the light and dark colors as they work.

The Project

1. Put on an apron.

2. Select a sheet of construction paper and write your name on the back of it.

3. Use crayons to draw a picture on the front of the paper. To make this project work, be sure to press down on the crayons as hard as you can.

4. Choose one color of paint wash to brush all over your picture.

Follow-Up

Have the children share their pictures. What happened to the crayon picture when they brushed the paint wash over it? Ask the children to group themselves by what color of paint wash they used. Which color was used the most? If you wish, copy the additional worksheets on pages 40 and 41 for the children to complete in class or at home.

Crayon Resist

1. Put on apron

2. Write name on paper.

Michiko

3. Draw a picture with crayons.

4. Brush paint wash all over paper.

Name_____

Finish each picture.

Name_____

Connect the dots. Color the picture.

4 ● ● 5

2 ● 3 ●————————● 6 ● 7

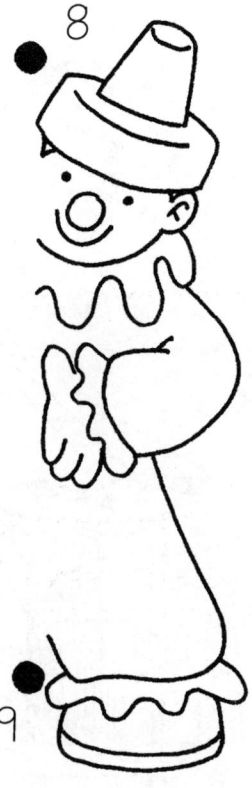

1

RED

8

10

9

Crayon Resist • Creation Station **41**

Crepe-Paper Design

Objectives

Develop creativity and small-motor skills.

Materials Needed

❏ crepe paper
❏ scissors
❏ bowl
❏ water
❏ paintbrush
❏ white construction paper
❏ pencil
❏ project worksheet

Setting Up the Station

• Cut various colors of crepe paper into squares.
• Fill a bowl with water.
• Set out the crepe-paper squares, the bowl of water, a paintbrush, white construction paper, and a pencil.
• Copy and display the project worksheet on page 43.

Introducing the Project

Talk about colors with your children. Ask them to name some of the colors they see around them. Let each child say his or her favorite color. Explain to the children the following project steps for making colorful designs.

The Project

1. Select a sheet of white construction paper and write your name on the back of it.

2. Use a paintbrush to brush water all over the paper.

3. Arrange crepe-paper squares all over the wet paper. Wait for the paper to dry a little.

4. Remove the crepe-paper squares to reveal the colorful design.

Follow-Up

Display the children's mosaics. Talk about the colors used. Are there any places were two colors blended together to make a third color? If you wish, copy the additional worksheets on pages 44 and 45 for the children to complete in class or at home.

Crepe-Paper Design

1. Write name on paper.

2. Brush on water.

3. Put on crepe-paper squares. Wait.

4. Remove squares.

Name_____

Color the picture. R=red Y=yellow G=green

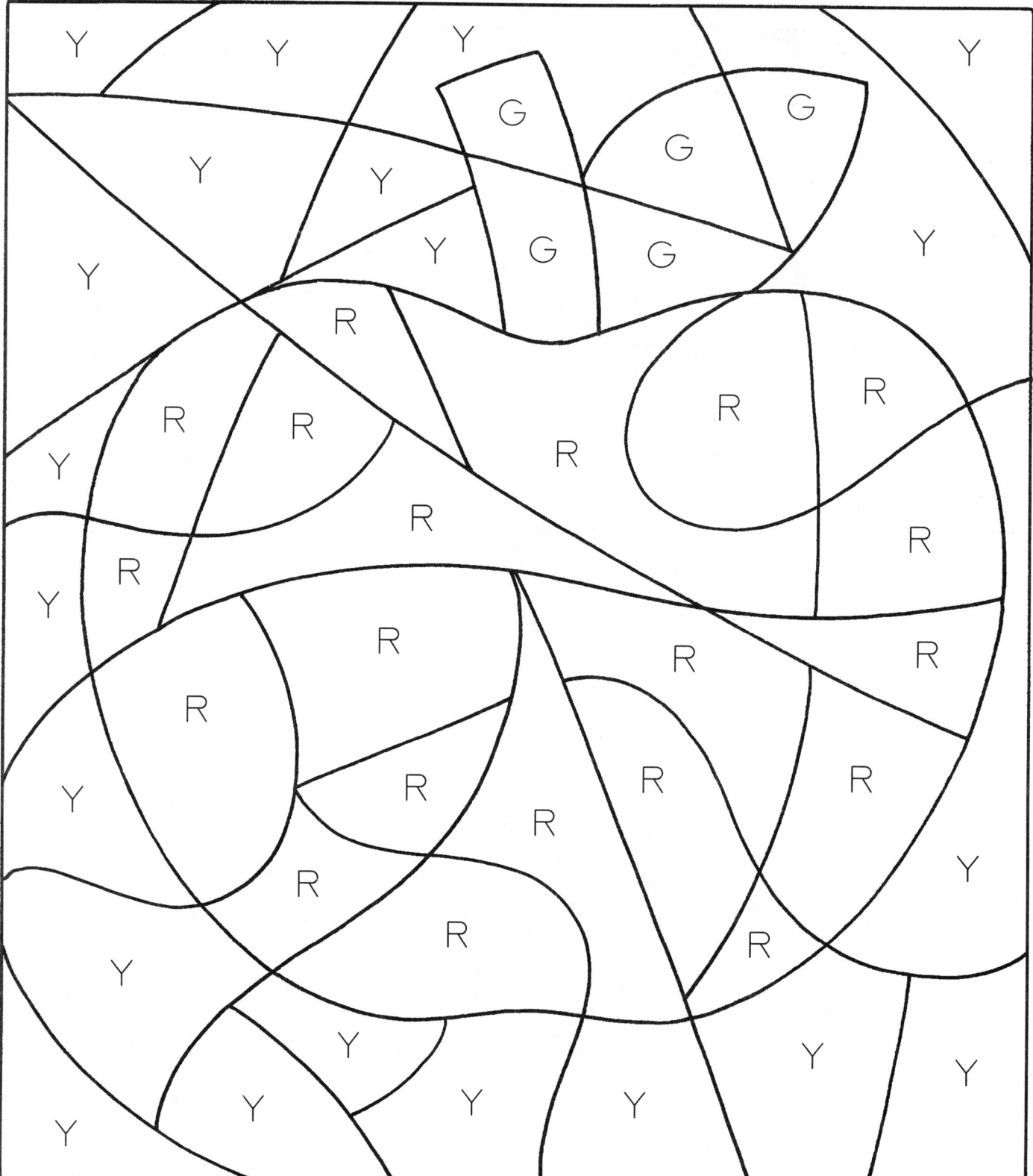

Name_____

Color each flower a different color.

Crown

Objectives

Practice cutting and gluing skills and develop creativity.

Materials Needed

❑ construction paper
❑ scissors
❑ gift-wrap
❑ pencil
❑ glue
❑ tape
❑ project worksheet

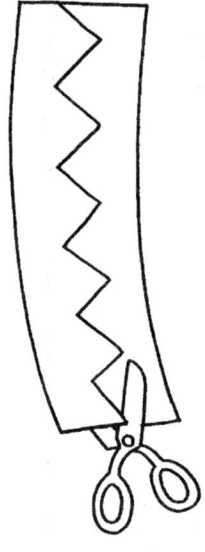

Setting Up the Station

• Cut crown shapes out of large sheets of construction paper.
• Cut small squares out of various kinds of gift-wrap (foil gift-wrap works especially well).
• Set out the crown shapes, gift-wrap squares, a pencil, glue, and tape.
• Copy and display the project worksheet on page 47.

Introducing the Project

Have your children watch as you cut a diamond shape, a circle shape, and a triangle shape out of the gift-wrap. Ask them to name the shapes. Explain how they will be using these shapes as you tell them the following project steps.

The Project

1. Select a crown shape and write your name on it.

2. Cut shapes out of the gift-wrap.

3. Arrange the paper shapes on your crown shape to make any design you would like.

4. Glue the shapes in place and set your crown aside to dry.

Follow-Up

Help the children adjust their crowns on their heads and securely tape the ends together. Have them take off their crowns and look at all the shapes. Which shape did they use the most? What colors can they see on their crowns? Let the children wear their crowns as they march around the room in a royal parade. If you wish, copy the additional worksheets on pages 48 and 49 for the children to complete in class or at home.

Crown

1. Write name on crown.

2. Cut out shapes.

3. Arrange shapes on crown.

4. Glue shapes in place.

Name_____

Color the shapes.

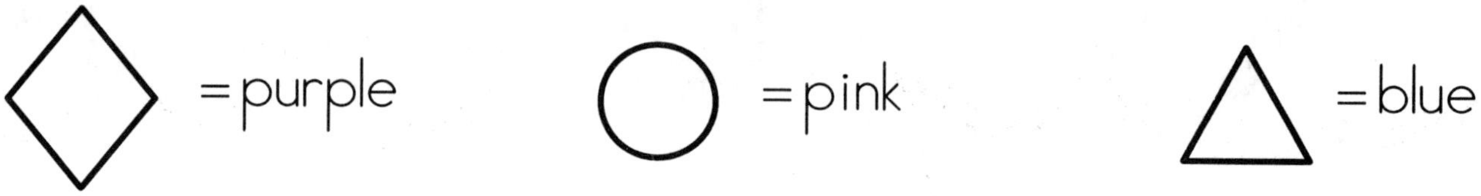

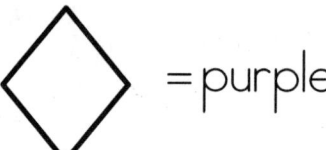 =purple   ◯ =pink   △ =blue

Name_____

Draw lines to connect the crowns that match.

Design a Hat

Objectives

Practice cutting and gluing skills and develop imagination and creativity.

Materials Needed

❑ pictures of hats
❑ paper plates
❑ scissors
❑ pencil
❑ glue
❑ collage materials
❑ project worksheet
❑ *Go, Dog, Go* by Dr. Seuss

Setting Up the Station

• Hang up pictures of hats in the station.
• Set out paper plates, scissors, a pencil, glue, and collage materials (crepe paper, ribbon, felt scraps, buttons, silk flowers, yarn scraps, etc.).
• Copy and display the project worksheet on page 51.

Introducing the Project

Read *Go, Dog, Go* by Dr. Suess to your children. Have them notice all the different kinds of hats as you read the story. Ask them to think about what kind of hat they might like to design as you explain the following project steps to them.

The Project

1. Fold a paper plate in half.
2. Cut out the center of the paper plate, leaving just the rim.
3. Write your name on the rim.
4. Arrange the collage materials on the rim and glue them in place.

Follow-Up

Plan a hat parade to another room for the children to show off their hats. If you wish, copy the additional worksheets on pages 52 and 53 for the children to complete in class or at home.

Design a Hat

1. Fold plate in half.

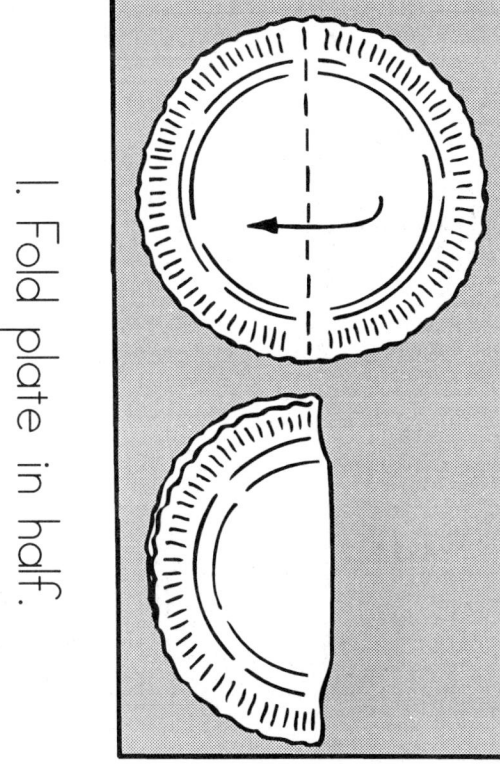

2. Cut out center.

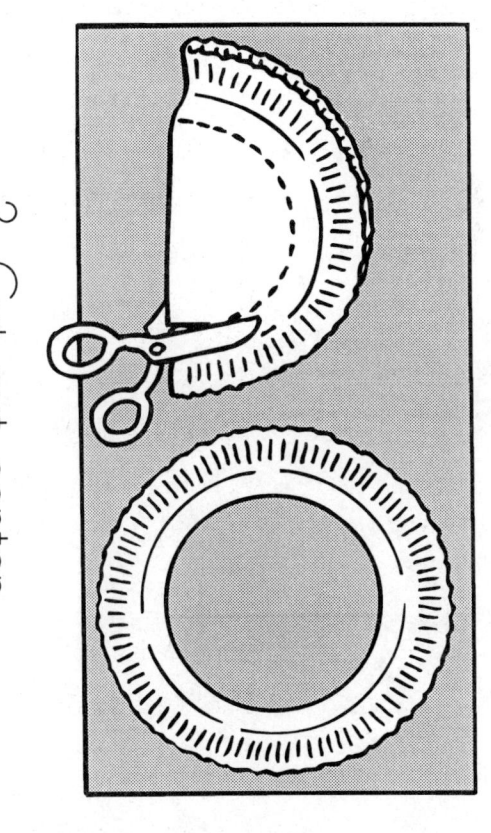

3. Write name.

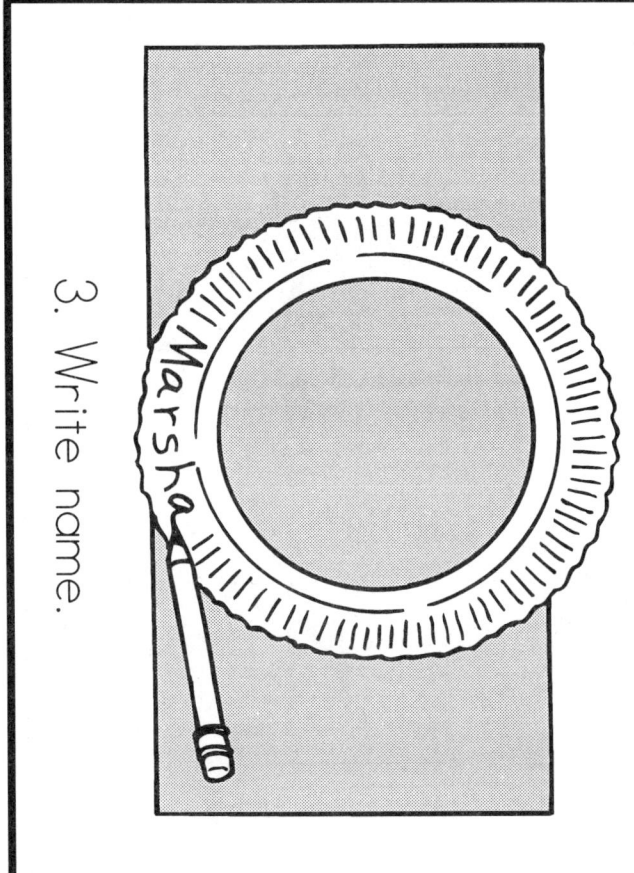

4. Decorate.

Design a Hat • Creation Station

Name_____

Draw a line from each hat to the worker who wears it.

Name_____

Decorate the hat.

Dot-o-Gram

Objectives

Develop problem-solving and small-motor skills.

Materials Needed

❑ dot-to-dot puzzles
❑ dot markers
❑ plain paper
❑ pencil
❑ project worksheet

Setting Up the Station

• Hang up several dot-to-dot puzzles in the station. Have some of them completed, some of them partially done, and some of them not done at all.

• Collect several nontoxic dot markers (similar to the kind used for playing bingo). These markers are often available at children's art supply stores.

• Set out the dot markers, plain paper, and a pencil.

• Copy and display the project worksheet on page 55.

Introducing the Project

Talk about dot-to-dot puzzles. Show some to your children. Talk about how the dots outline the picture. Ask them how they find out what the picture is. (By connecting the dots.) Explain to them the following project steps for making their own dot-to-dot pictures.

The Project

1. Select a sheet of paper.

2. Write your name on the back of the paper.

3. Use a dot marker to print dots all over the paper.

4. Use a pencil to connect the dots to make your picture or design.

Follow-Up

Have the children share their Dot-o-Grams with one another. What kinds of designs or pictures did they make? Using chalk, work together to make a giant Dot-o-Gram outside on the playground. If you wish, copy the additional worksheets on pages 56 and 57 for the children to complete in class or at home.

Dot-o-Gram

1. Choose paper.

2. Write name.

3. Make dots.

4. Connect dots.

Name_____

Count each set of dots and write the number in the box.

Name_____

Connect the black dots.

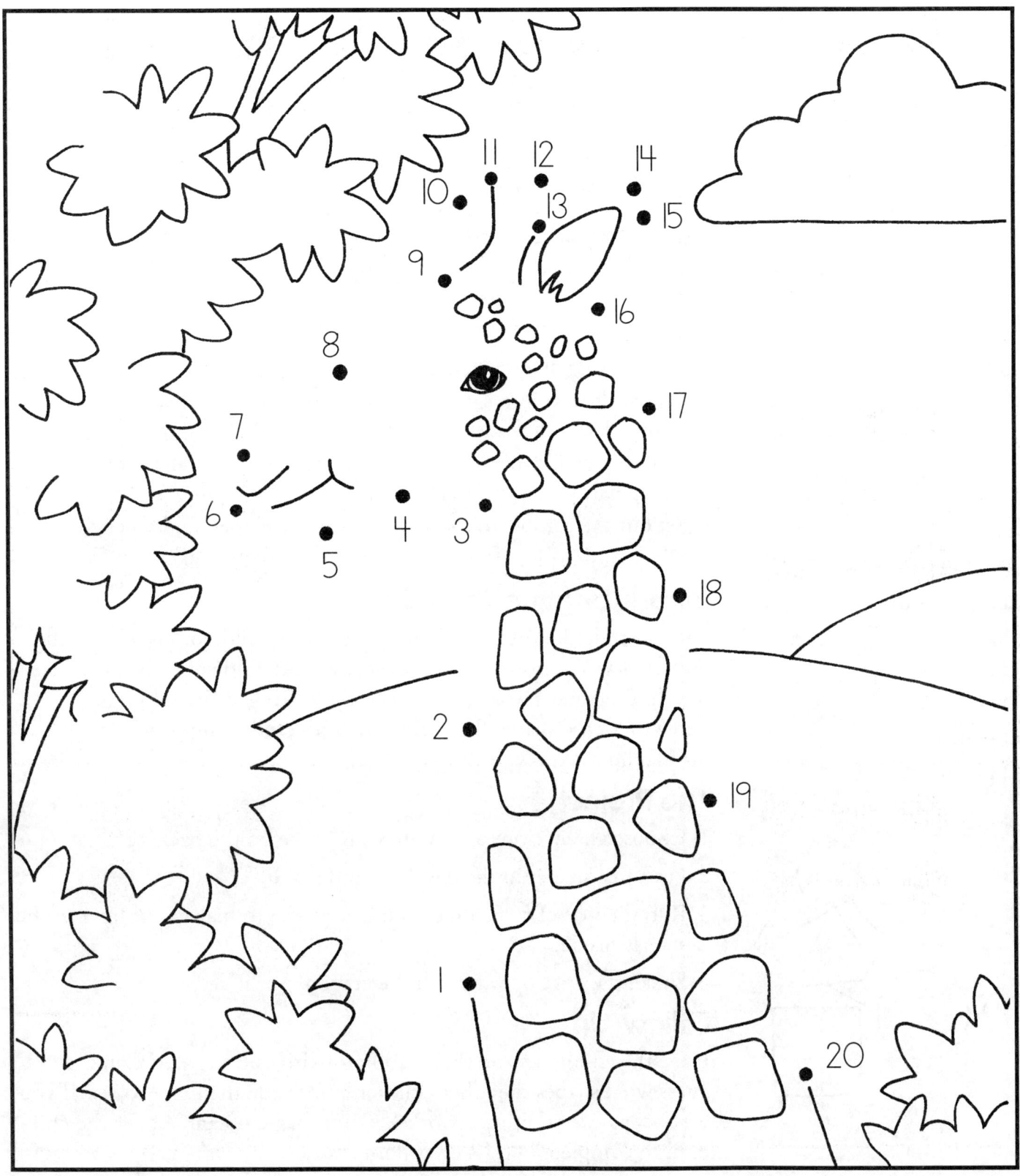

Envelope Rubbing

Objectives

Practice problem-solving skills and develop small-motor skills.

Materials Needed

❏ cardboard
❏ scissors
❏ crayons
❏ envelopes
❏ pencil
❏ project worksheet

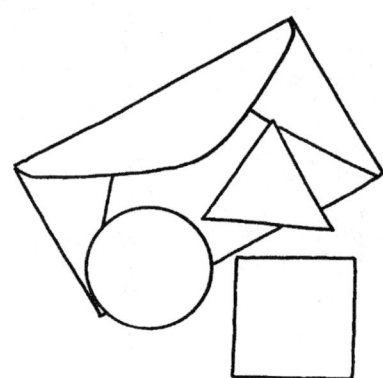

Setting Up the Station

• Cut cardboard into small familiar shapes such as circles, squares, triangles, rectangles, stars, diamonds, and hearts.
• Collect a variety of colors of crayons and remove their paper wrappers.
• Set out the cardboard shapes, crayons, envelopes, and a pencil.
• Copy and display the project worksheet on page 59.

Introducing the Project

Demonstrate the rubbing technique to your children. Put one of the shapes in an envelope and rub over it with the side of a crayon. Have the children guess what the shape is by looking at the rubbing. Show them the shape. Explain to them the following project steps for making their own rubbings.

The Project

1. Choose an envelope and write your name on the back of it.

2. Put three shapes in the envelope and seal it.

3. Rub the side of a crayon over the envelope to make a rubbing of the shapes inside.

4. Shake the envelope and rub the crayon over it again.

Follow-Up

Have the children share their rubbings with one another. Can they guess what shapes the other children put inside their envelopes? If you wish, copy the additional worksheets on pages 60 and 61 for the children to complete in class or at home.

Envelope Rubbing

1. Write name on envelope.

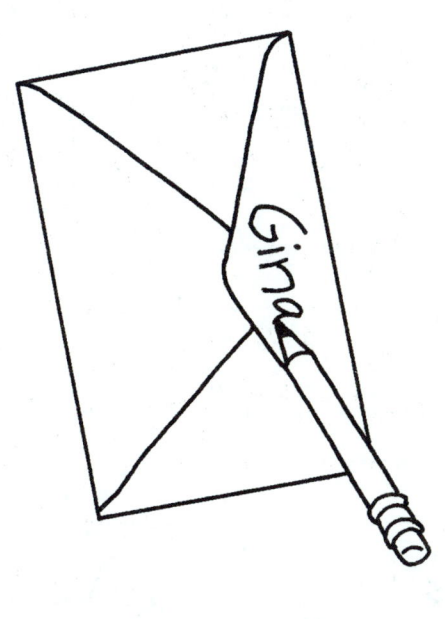

2. Put in 3 shapes.

3. Rub crayon over envelope.

4. Shake and rub again.

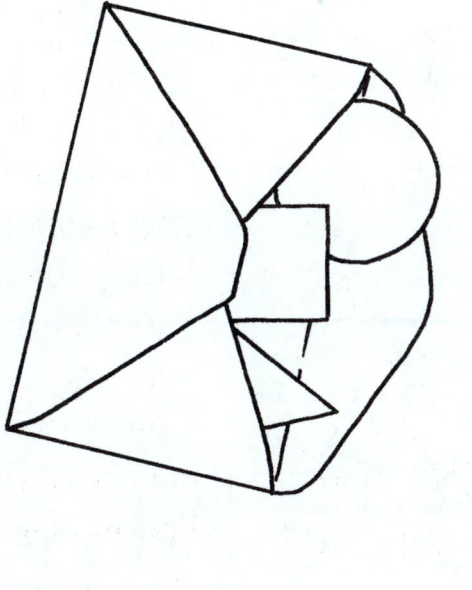

Name_____

For each box, cross out the shape that does not match.

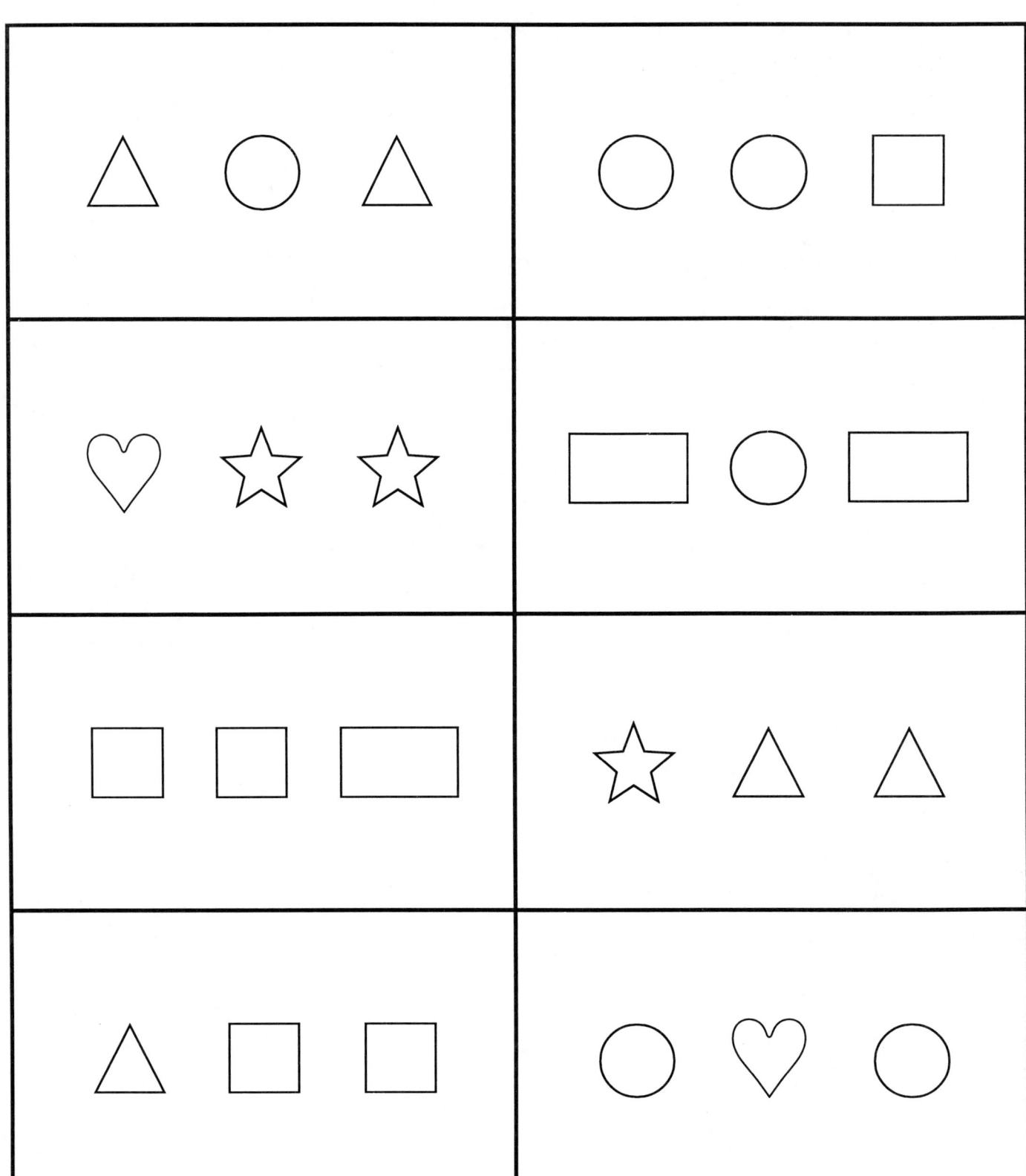

Name_____

Draw a line from each object to its missing part.

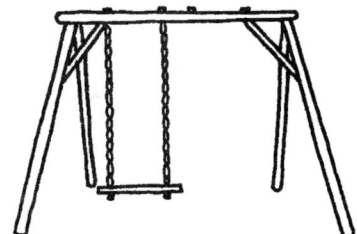
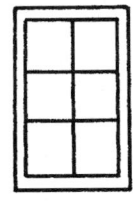

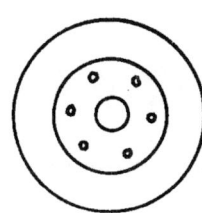

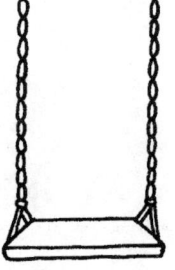

Flower Vase

Objectives

Develop creativity and small-motor skills.

Materials Needed

☐ flowers in vases
☐ glass jars
☐ tissue paper
☐ scissors
☐ glue
☐ bowl
☐ paintbrush
☐ self-stick labels
☐ pencil
☐ artificial flowers
☐ project worksheet

Setting Up the Station

- At the station, put out one or two vases with flowers.
- Collect a glass jar for each child.
- Cut various colors of tissue paper into small squares.
- Pour a small amount of glue into a bowl.
- Set out the jars, tissue paper squares, the bowl of glue, a paintbrush, self-stick labels, and a pencil.
- Collect artificial flowers for the children to arrange in their vases at a later time.
- Copy and display the project worksheet on page 63.

Introducing the Project

Talk about all the different kinds of flowers there are. Ask your children to think of all the different colors of flowers they have seen. What are some of the names? Show them the vases of flowers in the station. Why do cut flowers need a vase? Explain to them the following project steps for making vases for their own beautiful flowers.

The Project

1. Choose one of the glass jars.

2. Write your name on a self-stick label and put it on the bottom of the jar.

3. Brush glue all over the jar.

4. Stick tissue paper squares all over the glue.

Follow-Up

When the glue on the vases has dried, give the children a few artificial flowers to arrange in their vases. Let them take their vases home. If you wish, copy the additional worksheets on pages 64 and 65 for the children to complete in class or at home.

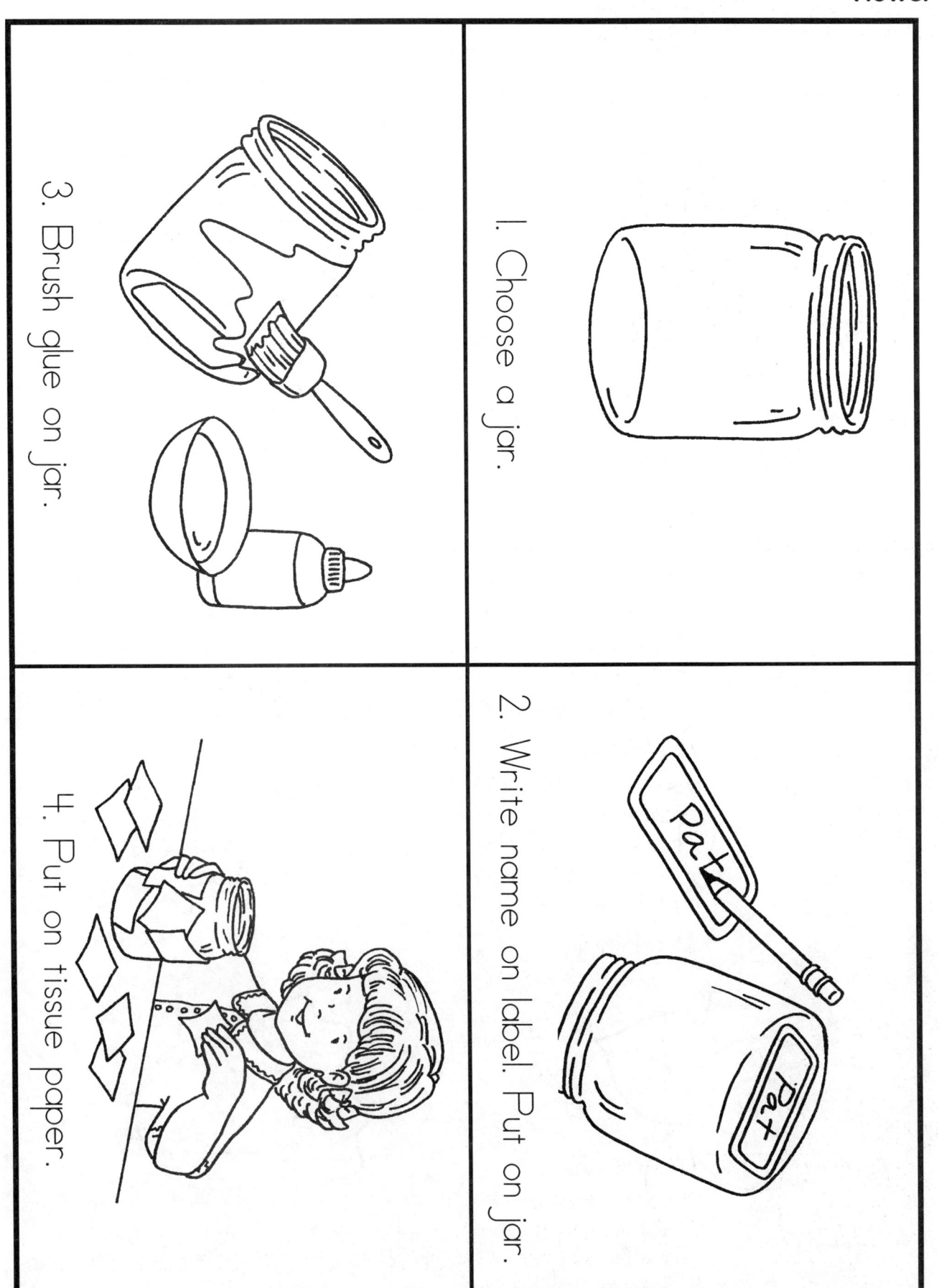

Flower Vase

1. Choose a jar.

2. Write name on label. Put on jar.

3. Brush glue on jar.

4. Put on tissue paper.

Name_____

Count the petals on each flower and write the number on the line.

Name_____

For each row, color the flowers that match.

Greeting Card

Objectives

Practice gluing skills and develop creativity.

Materials Needed

❏ greeting cards
❏ decorative materials
❏ glue
❏ bowl
❏ paintbrush
❏ construction paper
❏ crayons
❏ pencil
❏ large envelopes
❏ project worksheet

Setting Up the Station

- Hang up several greeting cards in the station.
- Collect a variety of decorative materials (yarn scraps, sequins, dried flowers, shiny paper scraps, etc.).
- Pour a small amount of glue into a bowl.
- Set out the decorative materials, the bowl of glue, a paintbrush, construction paper, crayons, and a pencil.
- Collect large envelopes for the completed cards.
- Copy and display the project worksheet on page 67.

Introducing the Project

Show your children some of the greeting cards. Talk about why people send cards to one another. Have the children think of greeting card messages they might like to write. Explain to them the following project steps for making their own special greeting cards.

The Project

1. Choose a sheet of construction paper and fold it in half.
2. On the inside of the card, write or draw a message and sign your name.
3. Brush glue on the front of the card.
4. Select some collage decorations and arrange them on the glue.

Follow-Up

After the glue has dried, let the children share their cards with the group. Help them put their cards in envelopes and write the names of the recipients on the front. If you wish, copy the additional worksheets on pages 68 and 69 for the children to complete in class or at home.

Greeting Card

1. Fold paper in half.

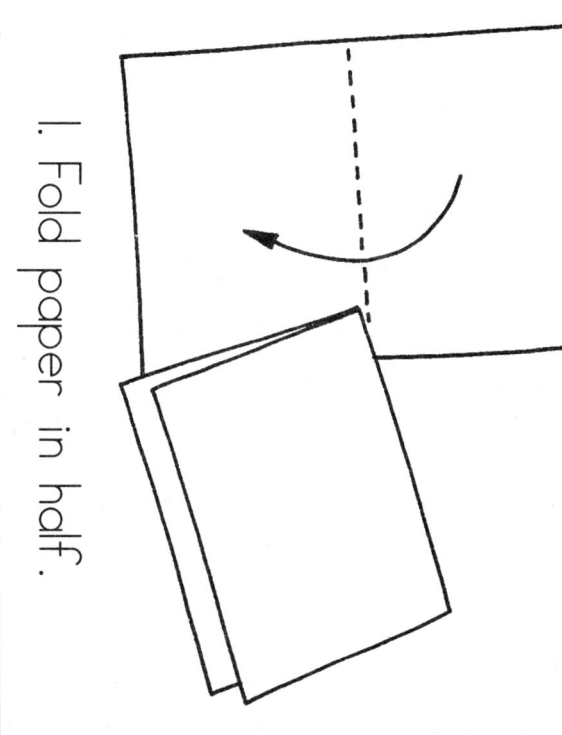

3. Brush glue on front.

2. Write message and name inside.

I love you! Kim

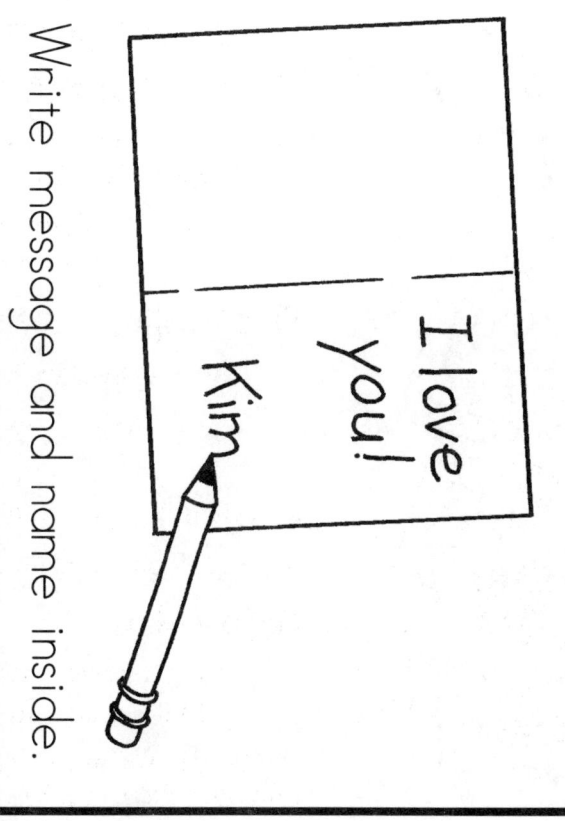

4. Put on decorations.

Name_____

Draw lines to connect the cards that match.

Name_____

Help the mail carrier deliver the letter.

Hidden Picture Card

Objectives

Practice using a hole punch and develop imagination and problem-solving skills.

Materials Needed

❑ construction paper
❑ ruler
❑ scissors
❑ magazines
❑ pencil
❑ hole punch
❑ glue
❑ project worksheet

Setting Up the Station

• Cut construction paper in half to make 6-by-9-inch rectangles.

• Tear interesting pictures out of magazines. Cut the pictures into 6-by-4-inch rectangles.

• Set out the construction paper rectangles, magazine pictures, a pencil, a hole punch, and glue.

• Prepare one of the cards for an example.

• Copy and display the project worksheet on page 71.

Introducing the Project

Show your children the card you prepared as an example. Have them look carefully through the holes. Can they tell what picture is inside? Open up the card. Did they guess right? Put another picture inside the card. Let them look through the holes and guess again. Explain to the children the following project steps for making their own Hidden Picture Cards.

The Project

1. Select a piece of construction paper and write your name on the back.

2. Fold the construction paper in half.

3. Select a magazine picture and glue it on the inside of the card.

4. Punch holes on the other half of the card.

Follow-Up

Let the children share their cards with others. Let them guess what each others' pictures are before opening up the cards. If you wish, copy the additional worksheets on pages 72 and 73 for the children to complete in class or at home.

Hidden Picture Card

1. Write name on paper.

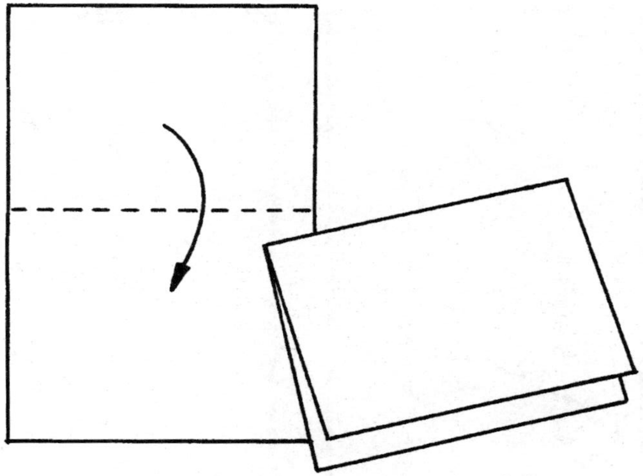

Jason

2. Fold paper in half.

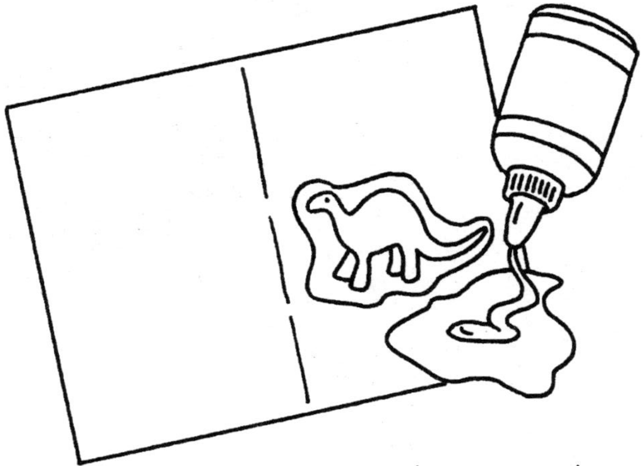

3. Glue picture inside card.

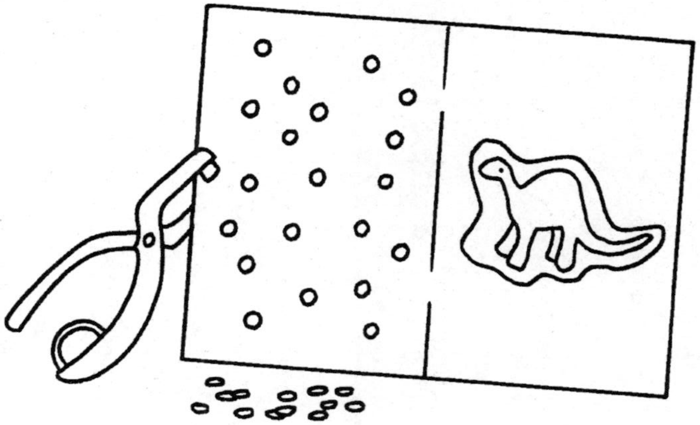

4. Punch holes.

Name_____

Cut out the animal tails at the bottom of the page. Paste them next to the matching animal heads.

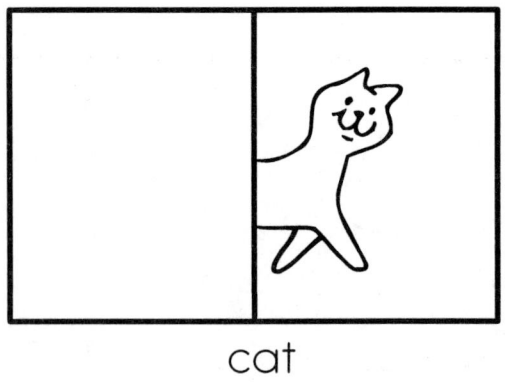

cat

horse

rabbit

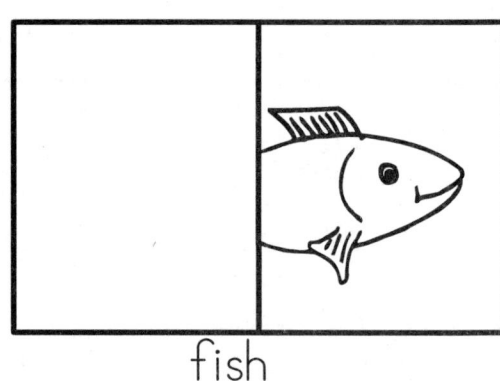

fish

Name_____

Find these objects in the picture and circle them.

License Plate Rubbing

Objectives

Practice making rubbings.

Materials Needed

❑ old license plates
❑ large crayons
❑ plain paper
❑ pencil
❑ project worksheet

Setting Up the Station

• Find two or three old license plates.
• Collect a variety of colors of large crayons. Remove the wrappers from the crayons.
• Set out the license plates, crayons, plain paper, and a pencil.
• Copy and display the project worksheet on page 75.

Introducing the Project

Show your children the license plates. Let them feel the raised surfaces on the plates. Put a sheet of paper over one of the license plates and rub a crayon across it. Have the children watch as the numbers and letters on the plate get transferred to the paper. Explain to them the following project steps for making their own rubbings.

The Project

1. Choose a license plate and set it on the table in front of you.
2. Write your name on a piece of paper.
3. Put the paper over the license plate.
4. Use the side of a crayon to rub across the paper on top of the license plate.

Follow-Up

Let the children share their rubbings with the class. Have them group themselves according to which license plate they used. Ask each group to say the letters and numbers on their rubbings. If you wish, copy the additional worksheets on pages 76 and 77 for the children to complete in class or at home.

License Plate Rubbing

1. Choose a license plate.

2. Write name on paper.

Malik

3. Put paper over license plate.

Malik

4. Rub crayon over paper.

Malik

Name_____

Draw a line connecting each set of letters to its matching license plate.

O P S

A B C

D F B

X Y Z

J K L

M P Q

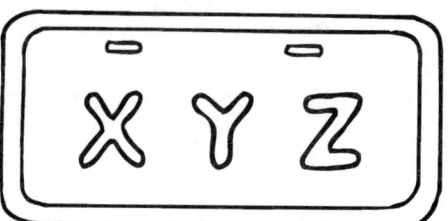

Name_____

For each row, circle the numbers that match the ones on the license plate.

License Plate					
2 4 5	5	4	6	2	9
1 7 3	2	3	7	4	1
6 4 8	4	2	6	8	0
9 3 6	3	7	1	9	6
1 8 2	1	9	8	4	2
0 7 5	9	0	2	7	5

Make-a-Game

Objectives

Practice rubber-stamping and cutting skills and develop problem-solving skills.

Materials Needed

- ❑ ready-made concentration game
- ❑ index cards
- ❑ rubber stamps
- ❑ ink pads
- ❑ scissors
- ❑ resealable bags
- ❑ ballpoint pen
- ❑ project worksheet

Setting Up the Station

- Find a ready-made concentration game and put it in the station.
- Set out unlined index cards, rubber stamps, ink pads, scissors, resealable bags, and a ballpoint pen.
- Copy and display the project worksheet on page 79.

Introducing the Project

Show your children the ready-made concentration game. Try playing it as a group. Explain to them the following project steps for making their own concentration games.

The Project

1. Choose one index card and print the same rubber-stamp design on each end of the card.
2. Cut the card in half.
3. Repeat five times, using a different rubber stamp each time.
4. Use the pen to write your name on a resealable bag. Put the cards in the bag.

Follow-Up

Divide the children into pairs. Have the pairs play concentration with their game cards, using first one child's cards and then the other's. If you wish, copy the additional worksheets on pages 80 and 81 for the children to complete in class or at home.

Make-a-Game

1. Stamp design 2 times on one card.

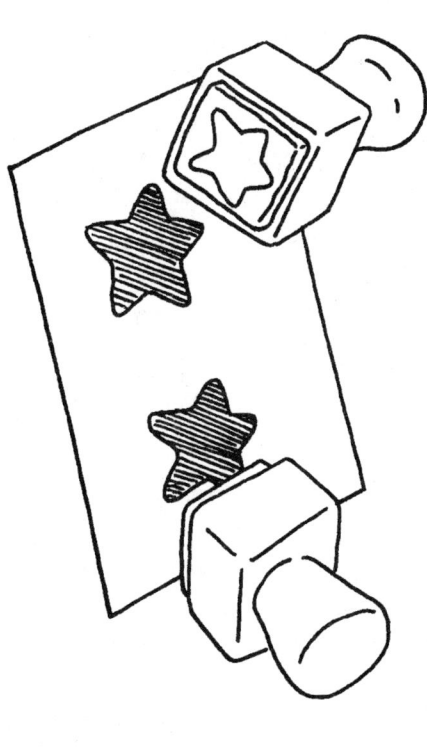

2. Cut card in half.

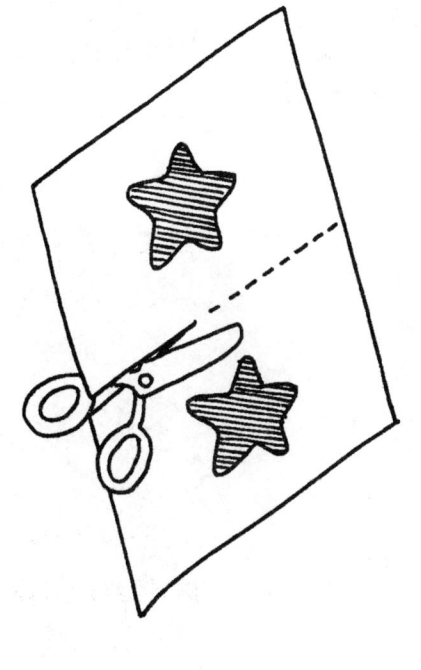

3. Repeat 5 times.

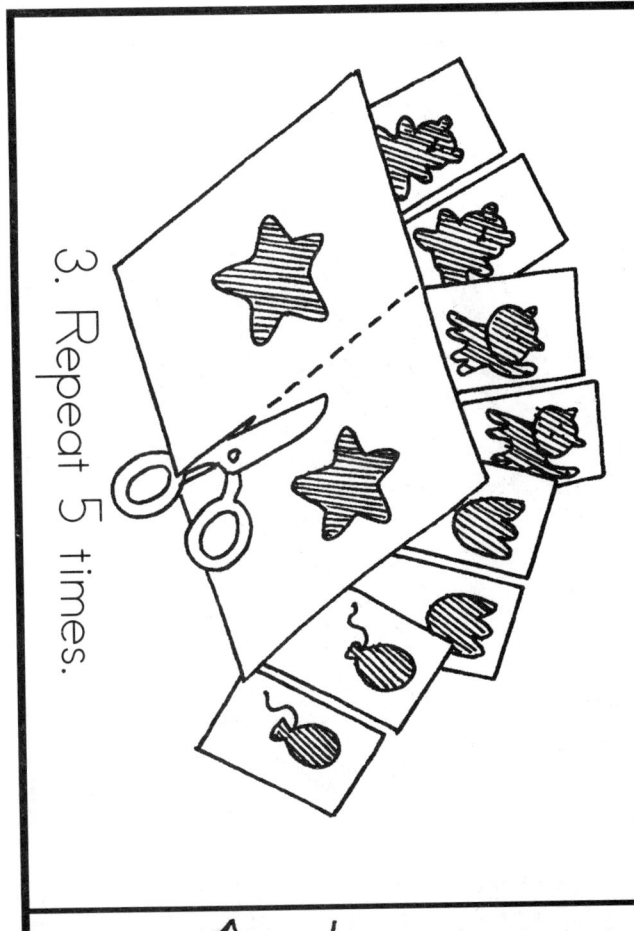

4. Write name on bag. Put in cards.

Name_____

Color the pairs that match.

Name_____

Help the girl find the path that leads to her twin.

Moonscape

Objectives

Practice gluing skills and develop creativity and small-motor skills.

Materials Needed

❑ moon pictures
❑ paper plates
❑ aluminum foil
❑ dried beans
❑ glue
❑ bowl
❑ paintbrush
❑ pencil
❑ project worksheet

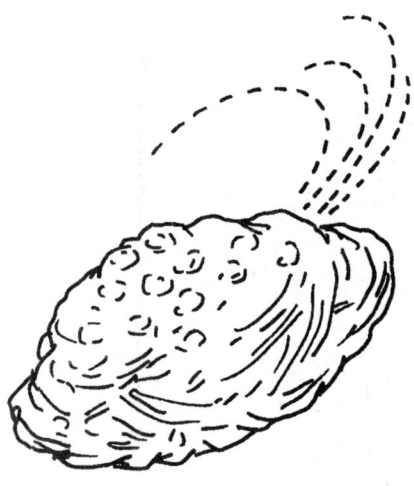

Setting Up the Station

- Hang up pictures of the moon, especially ones showing the moon's bumpy surface.
- Find heavy, cardboard-style paper plates of any size.
- Tear aluminum foil into squares about 2 inches larger than the paper plates.
- Put a small amount of glue into a bowl.
- Set out the paper plates, foil squares, dried beans, the bowl of glue, a paintbrush, and a pencil.
- Copy and display the project worksheet on page 83.

Introducing the Project

Show your children the pictures of the moon. Have them look carefully at the moon's surface. Does it look smooth or bumpy? Explain to the children the following project steps for making their own bumpy Moonscapes.

The Project

1. Take a paper plate and write your name on the front.
2. Turn the plate over and brush glue all over the bottom of the plate.
3. Arrange the beans on the glue and wait a few moments for the glue to dry.
4. Cover the bumpy bean surface of the plate with aluminum foil and press the foil around the beans.

Follow-Up

Arrange the children's Moonscapes on a bulletin board in a circle to make one large Moonscape. If you wish, copy the additional worksheets on pages 84 and 85 for the children to complete in class or at home.

Moonscape

1. Write name on plate.

2. Turn plate over and brush on glue.

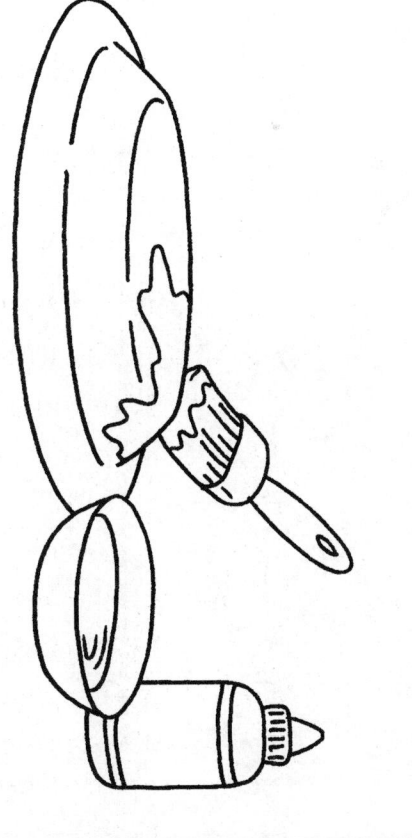

3. Put beans on glue. Wait.

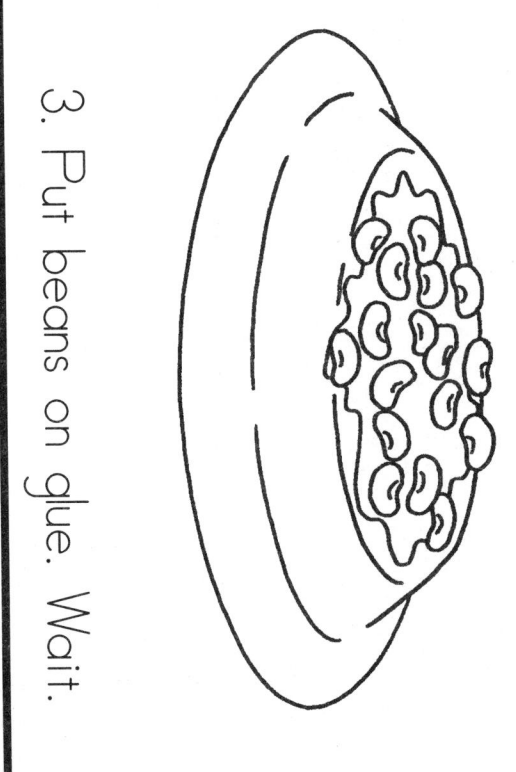

4. Cover plate and beans with foil.

Name_____

Cut out the story squares at the bottom of the page.
Glue them in order on the numbered squares.

1	2	3

Name_____

Trace the craters on the moon. Color the picture.

My Own Book

Objectives

Practice gluing and writing skills.

Materials Needed

❑ construction paper
❑ scissors
❑ stapler
❑ magazines
❑ pencil
❑ glue
❑ project worksheet

Setting Up the Station

• Cut sheets of construction paper in half. Make a book for each child by putting six half sheets of construction paper together and stapling them on the left-hand side.

• From magazines, cut out pictures of things the children like. Include pictures of people, animals, foods, activities, flowers, toys, etc.

• Set out the prepared books, the magazine pictures, a pencil, and glue.

• Copy and display the project worksheet on page 87.

Introducing the Project

Talk about things your children like. Ask each child to name one of his or her favorite things. Does everyone like the same thing? Why or why not? Explain to the children the following project steps for making a book of their most favorite things.

The Project

1. Select one of the ready-made books.

2. Write "My Favorite Things" and your name on the cover of the book.

3. Choose your favorite magazine pictures.

4. Glue the pictures to the pages in your book.

Follow-Up

Divide the children into pairs. Let the pairs take turns "reading" their books to each other. If you wish, copy the additional worksheets on pages 88 and 89 for the children to complete in class or at home.

My Own Book

1. Select a book.

2. Write "My Favorite Things" and name on cover.

3. Choose pictures.

4. Glue a picture on each page.

Name_____

Draw your favorite present.

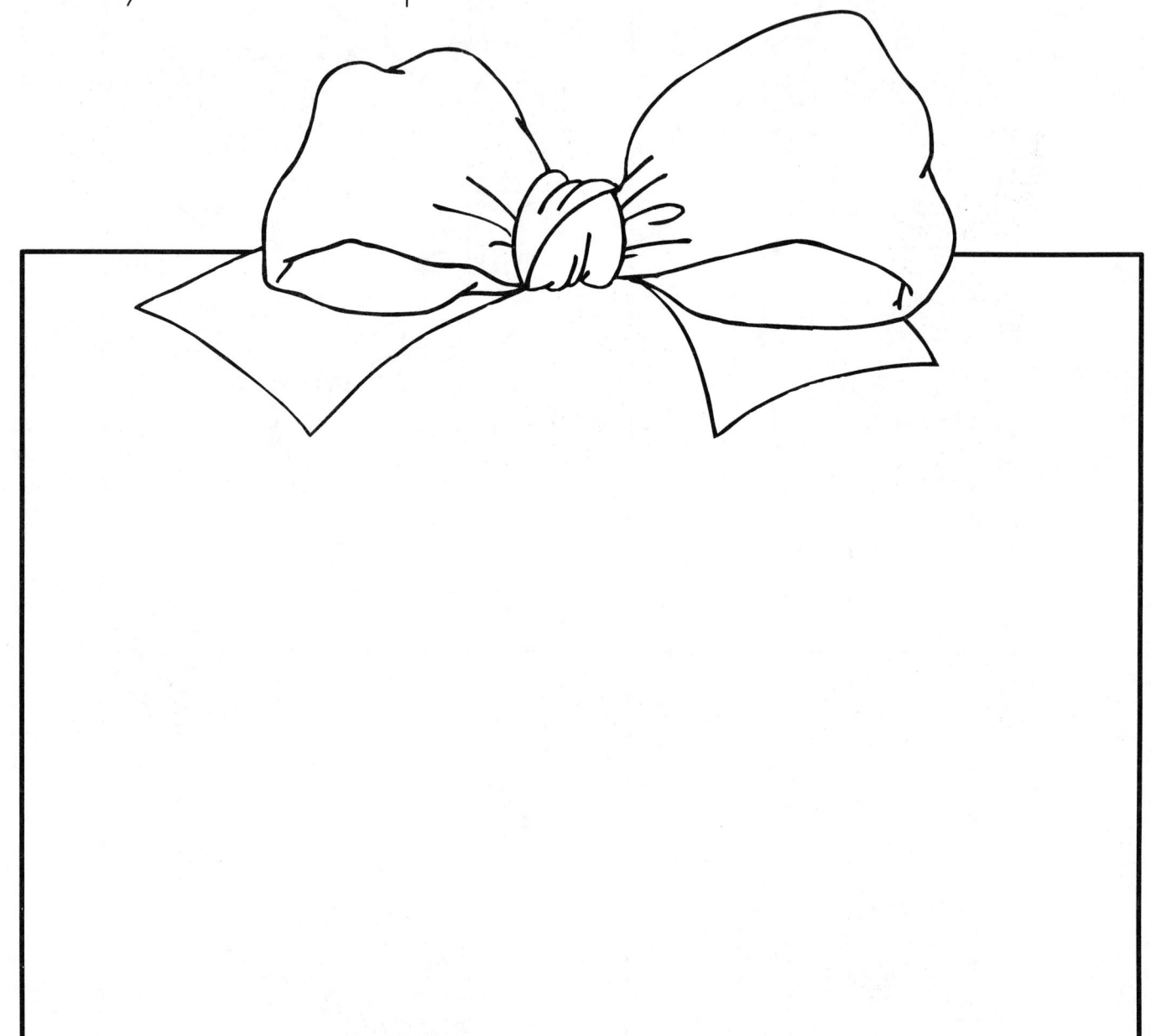

Name_____

Circle the things you like to do.

Necklace

Objectives

Practice cutting and stringing skills and develop patterning skills.

Materials Needed

❑ necklaces
❑ straws
❑ yarn
❑ scissors
❑ glue
❑ waxed paper
❑ project worksheet

Setting Up the Station

- Hang up necklaces of all kinds in the station. Try to include some colorful necklaces with beads arranged in patterns.
- Collect two different colors of plastic drinking straws. Make sure each color of straw has the same diameter opening. You will need one straw of each color for each child.
- Cut yarn into 2-foot lengths. Dip one end of each piece into glue. Place on waxed paper and allow the glue to dry. This makes a good "needle."
- Set out the straws and yarn pieces.
- Copy and display the project worksheet on page 91.

Introducing the Project

Show your children the necklaces. Which one is their favorite? What colors are the necklaces? Can anyone find a necklace with a bead pattern? Talk about the pattern. Explain to the children the following project steps for making their own necklaces. Encourage them to think about a pattern they might like to make with the straw "beads."

The Project

1. Choose a piece of yarn and one straw of each color.

2. Cut the straws into the lengths you want: short or long, or both.

3. String the straw pieces onto the yarn using the "needle." Put the straw pieces on so they make a pattern.

4. Tie the ends of the yarn together.

Follow-Up

Let the children wear their necklaces. Have them tell you the patterns they used. Did anyone use the same pattern? Ask them to count the number of straw pieces on their necklaces. Which necklace has the most pieces? Which one has the least? Do any of them have the same number? If you wish, copy the additional worksheets on pages 92 and 93 for the children to complete in class or at home.

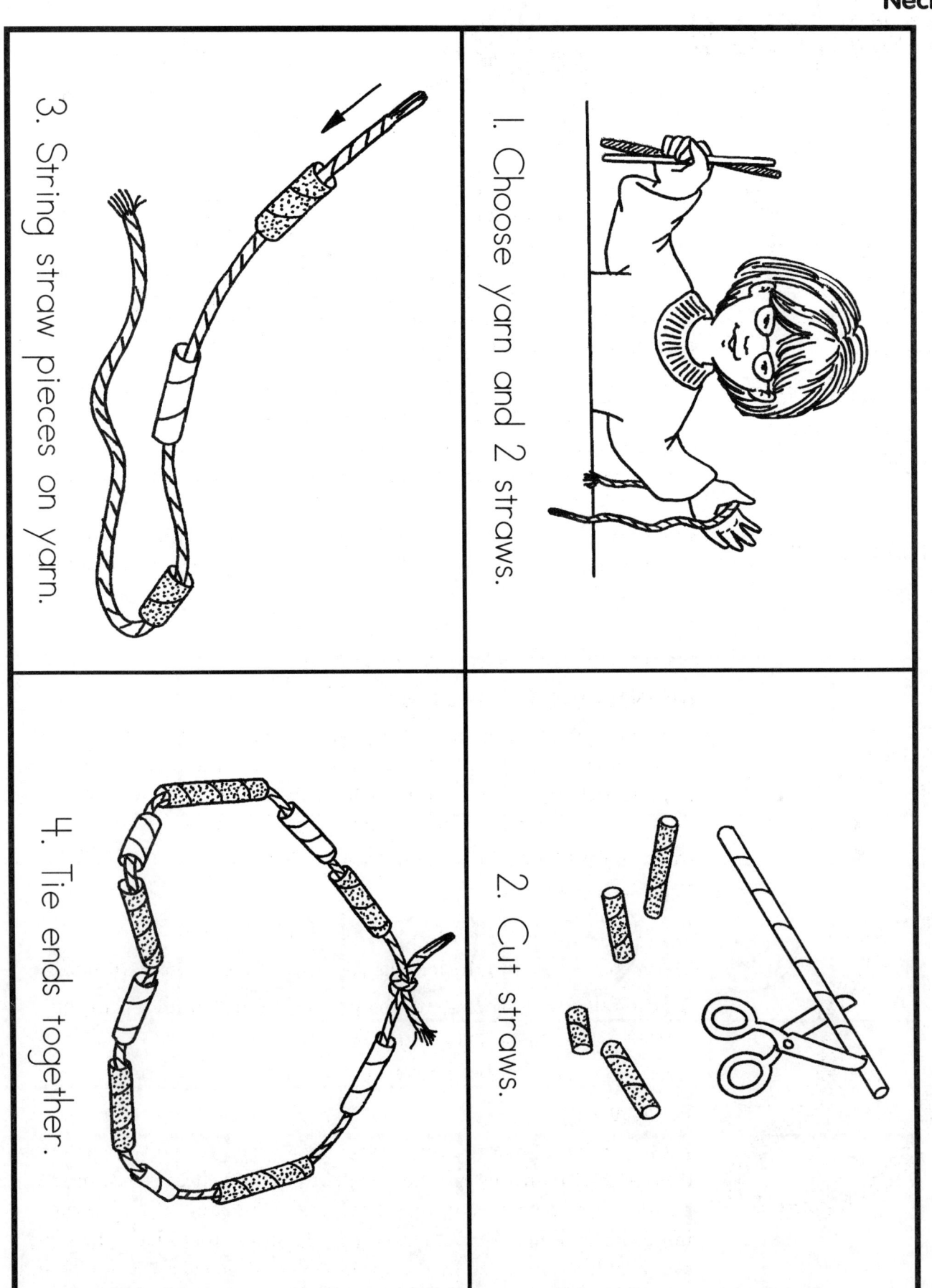

3. String straw pieces on yarn.

1. Choose yarn and 2 straws.

4. Tie ends together.

2. Cut straws.

Necklace

Name_____

Cut out the squares at the bottom of the page. Look at the pattern in each row and glue on the missing part.

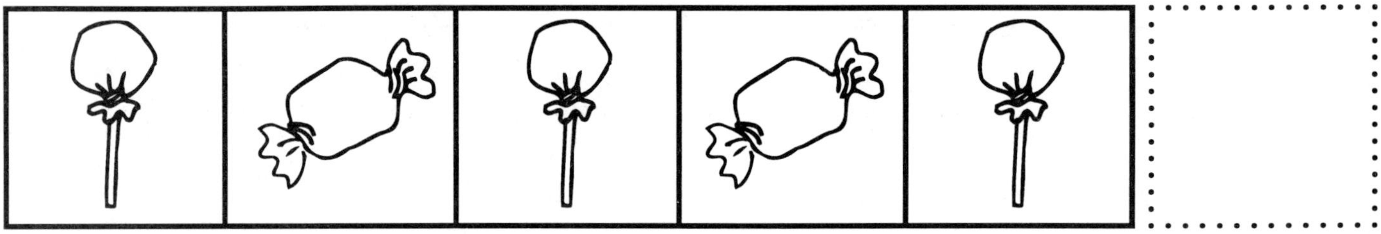

Name_____

For each box, circle the set with less.

Nylon Snake

Objectives

Practice cutting, gluing, and small-motor skills.

Materials Needed

❏ snake pictures
❏ pantyhose
❏ scissors
❏ newspaper
❏ twist ties
❏ felt scraps
❏ glue
❏ project worksheet

Setting Up the Station

- Hang up pictures of snakes.
- Cut the legs off old, clean pantyhose. You will need one nylon leg for each child.
- Set out the nylon legs, scissors, newspaper, twist ties, felt scraps, and glue.
- Copy and display the project worksheet on page 95.

Introducing the Project

Show your children the snake pictures. Encourage them to think of ways to describe the snakes. Point out the snakes' eyes and tongues. Explain the following steps to the children, so they can make their own Nylon Snakes.

The Project

1. Crumple the newspaper.
2. Stuff the newspaper into the nylon leg.
3. Secure the open end of the nylon leg with a twist tie.
4. Cut out felt eye and tongue shapes and glue them in place.

Follow-Up

Have the children introduce their snakes to the class. Can they think of names for their snakes? Display the snakes all around the room. If you wish, copy the additional worksheets on pages 96 and 97 for the children to complete in class or at home.

Nylon Snake

3. Fasten with twist tie.

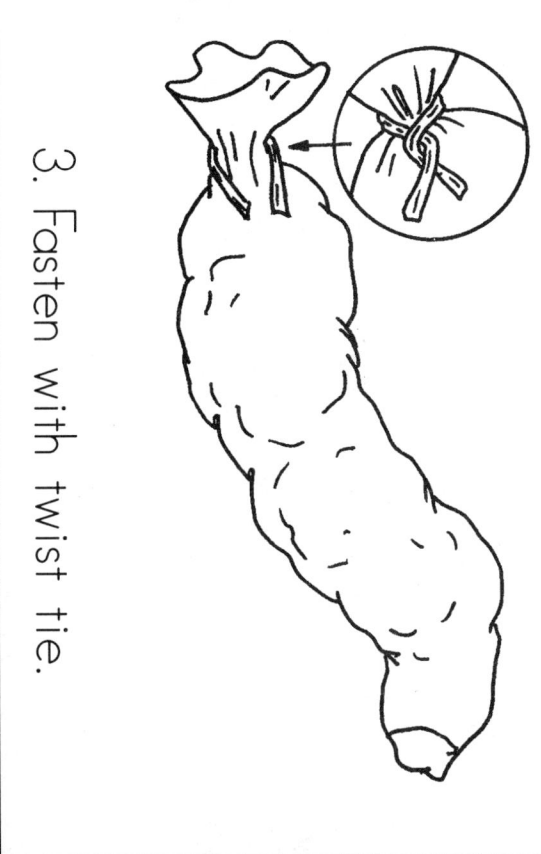

1. Crumple newspaper.

4. Add eyes and tongue.

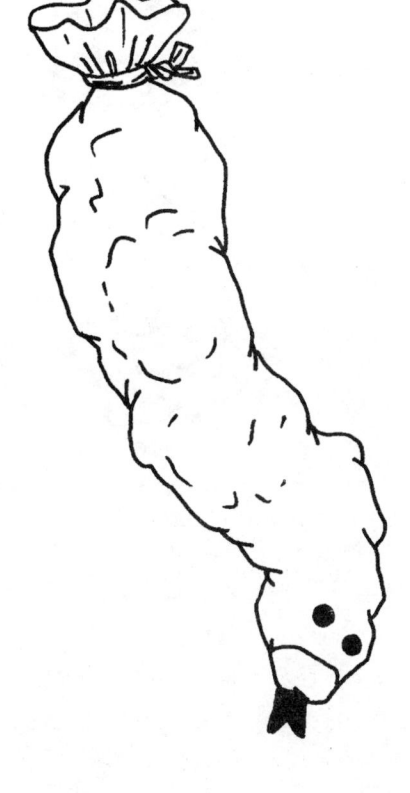

2. Stuff nylon with newspaper.

Name_____

Draw lines to connect the snakes that match.

Name_____

Color the snake's skin in a pattern.

Octopus

Objectives

Practice cutting and tracing skills.

Materials Needed

- ❑ octopus picture
- ❑ octopus pattern worksheet
- ❑ scissors
- ❑ black crayon
- ❑ tape
- ❑ pencil
- ❑ project worksheet

Setting Up the Station

- Hang up a picture of an octopus in the station.
- Make a copy of the octopus pattern worksheet on page 100 for each child. (If you wish, cover up the extra text on the page before copying.)
- Set out the copies of the octopus pattern, scissors, a black crayon, tape, and a pencil.
- Copy and display the project worksheet on page 99.

Introducing the Project

Show your children the picture of an octopus. Let them help you count the legs on it. Explain to them the following project steps for making a paper octopus.

The Project

1. Select a copy of the octopus pattern and cut along the dotted lines.

2. Use the black crayon to trace the eyes and mouth line.

3. Write your name on the back of the octopus.

4. Roll the paper into a cylinder and tape the ends together.

Follow-Up

Let each child hold his or her octopus like a puppet while you read a story or sing a song about living in the ocean. Have each child think of a name for his or her octopus. If you wish, copy the additional worksheet on page 101 for the children to complete in class or at home.

Octopus

1. Cut pattern on dotted lines.

2. Trace eyes and mouth.

3. Write name on back.

Carmen

4. Roll and tape.

Name_____

Circle the things that belong in the sea.
Cross out the things that do not belong.

Pet Rock

Objectives

Practice painting and gluing skills.

Materials Needed

❏ rocks
❏ wiggly eyes
❏ tempera paint
❏ paint cups
❏ paper plates
❏ pencil
❏ paintbrushes
❏ glue
❏ project worksheet

Setting Up the Station

• Collect rocks (or have the children collect rocks) that are 2 to 4 inches in diameter. Be sure there is one rock per child.

• Obtain wiggly eyes from a crafts supply store. You will need two per child.

• Put several colors of tempera paint in paint cups.

• Set out the rocks, wiggly eyes, paint cups, paper plates, a pencil, paintbrushes, and glue.

• Copy and display the project worksheet on page 103.

Introducing the Project

Ask your children to tell you about their pets. How many children have a pet at home? How many would like to have a pet at home? Make a graph showing what kinds of pets the children like the best. Tell them they will be making their very own pets—Pet Rocks. Then explain the following project steps to them.

The Project

1. Write your name on a paper plate.

2. Select a rock that you like and put it on the paper plate.

3. Paint the rock any way you wish.

4. Glue on two wiggly eyes.

Follow-Up

After the paint has dried, let the children hold their new pets. Ask them to think of names for their pets. Let them take turns introducing their pets to the children sitting beside them. If you wish, copy the additional worksheets on pages 104 and 105 for the children to complete in class or at home.

Pet Rock

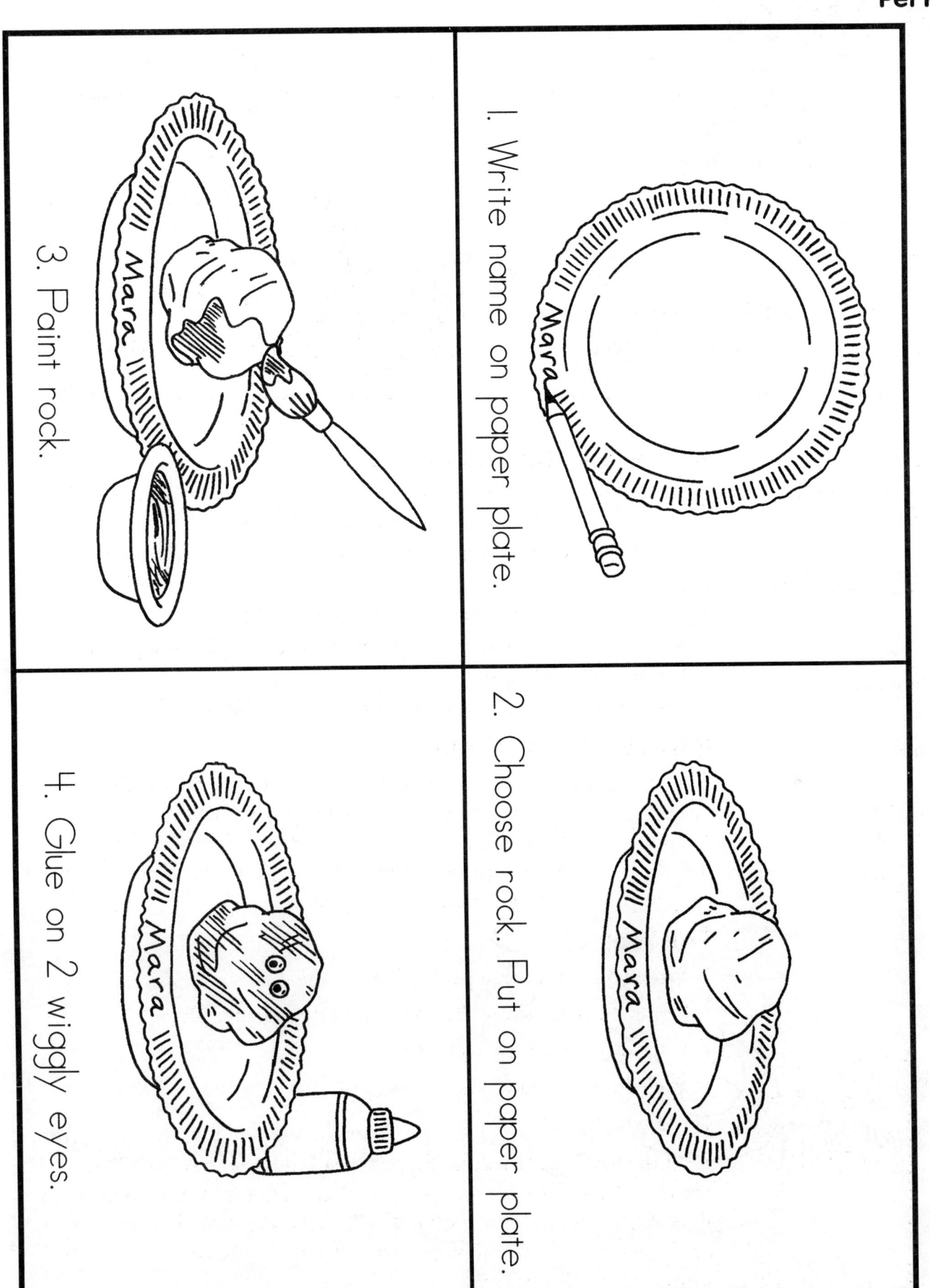

1. Write name on paper plate.

2. Choose rock. Put on paper plate.

3. Paint rock.

4. Glue on 2 wiggly eyes.

Name_____

Draw a home for the pet dog.

Name_____

For each box, count the pets and circle that number.

3　　4　　5

4　　5　　6

1　　2　　3

0　　1　　2

5　　6　　7

2　　3　　4

Pipe-Cleaner Animal

Objectives

Develop problem-solving, creative-thinking, and small-motor skills.

Materials Needed

❑ pictures of animals
❑ pipe cleaners
❑ scissors
❑ project worksheet

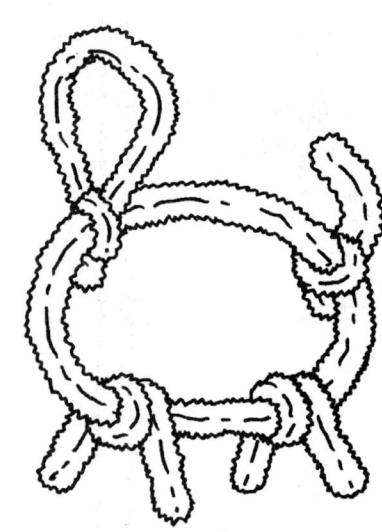

Setting Up the Station

• In the station, hang up pictures of four-legged animals.
• Cut colorful pipe cleaners in half and set them out.
• Copy and display the project worksheet on page 107.

Introducing the Project

Talk with your children about all the different animals they know. Ask them to identify the animals in the pictures. Explain to the children the following project steps for making a Pipe-Cleaner Animal. Tell them that they can follow these steps for making any kind of four-legged animal.

The Project

1. Select five pipe-cleaner halves.

2. Form one of the pipe cleaners into a circle or an oval to make a body shape.

3. Make the front legs with one pipe cleaner and the back legs with another.

4. Use the other two pipe cleaners to make a head and a tail to complete your animal.

Follow-Up

Set aside a special place for the children to display their Pipe-Cleaner Animals. Add appropriate props if you like. Encourage the children to give their animals names and to check on them daily. If you wish, copy the additional worksheets on pages 108 and 109 for the children to complete in class or at home.

Pipe-Cleaner Animal

1. Pick 5 pipe cleaners.

2. Make a body shape.

3. Make legs.

4. Make a head and a tail.

Name_____

Draw a line connecting each animal to where it lives.

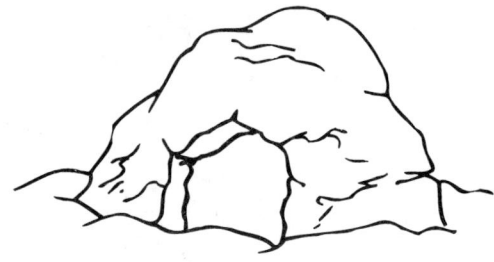

Name_____

Cut out the animals at the bottom of the page.
Glue only the farm animals inside the barn.

Polka Dot Picture

Objectives

Develop problem-solving and small-motor skills.

Materials Needed

- ❏ polka dot print
- ❏ construction paper
- ❏ ruler
- ❏ scissors
- ❏ glue
- ❏ bowl
- ❏ hole punch
- ❏ plastic containers
- ❏ white construction paper
- ❏ pencil
- ❏ paintbrush
- ❏ project worksheet

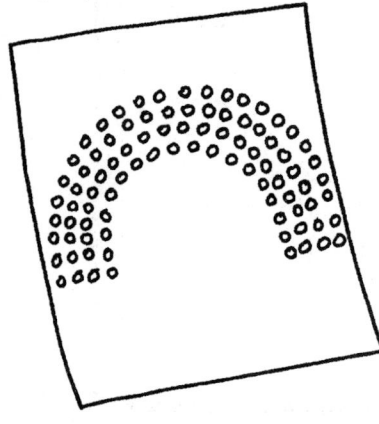

Setting Up the Station

- Find a polka dot print on fabric, gift-wrap, or a greeting card. Hang it up in the station.
- Cut a variety of colors of construction paper into 3-inch squares.
- Pour a small amount of glue into a bowl.
- Set out the construction paper squares, the bowl of glue, a hole punch, plastic containers, white construction paper, a pencil, and a paintbrush.
- Copy and display the project worksheet on page 111.

Introducing the Project

Show your children the polka dot print. Point out the circles that are found all over the print. Ask them to think about what kind of polka dot print they would like to make as you explain to them the following project steps.

The Project

1. Make dots by punching holes out of the colorful construction paper squares. Put each color of dot into a separate plastic container.

2. Select a sheet of white construction paper and write your name on the back.

3. Brush glue onto the paper.

4. Place the dots onto the glue to make your picture.

Follow-Up

Display the children's polka dot prints. Ask the children to describe their pictures. What colors of dots did they use? If you wish, copy the additional worksheets on pages 112 and 113 for the children to complete in class or at home.

Polka Dot Picture

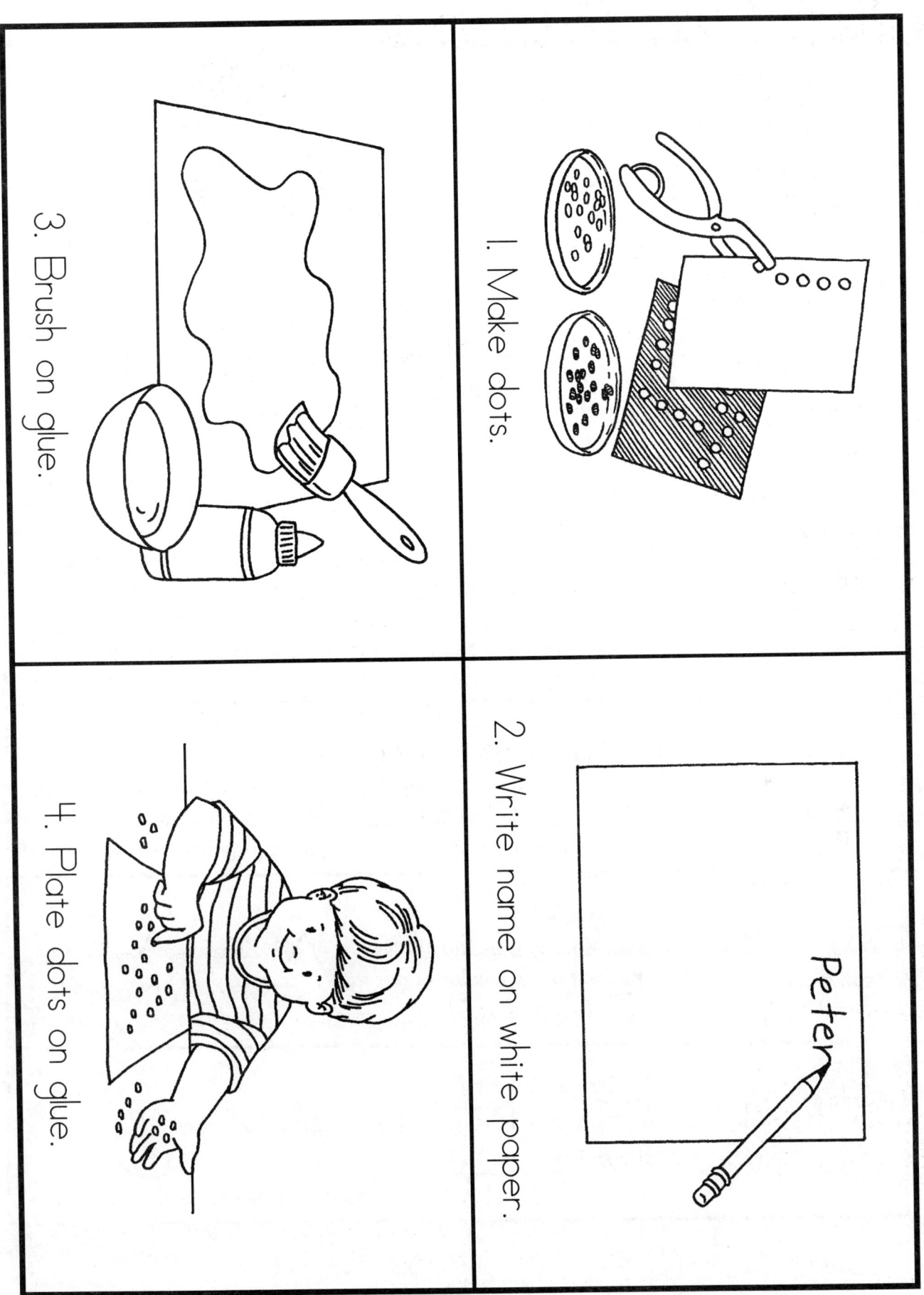

1. Make dots.

2. Write name on white paper.

Peter

3. Brush on glue.

4. Plate dots on glue.

Name_____

In each row, circle the shape that matches the first one.

Name_____

Color the dots.   R=red B=blue Y=yellow G=green

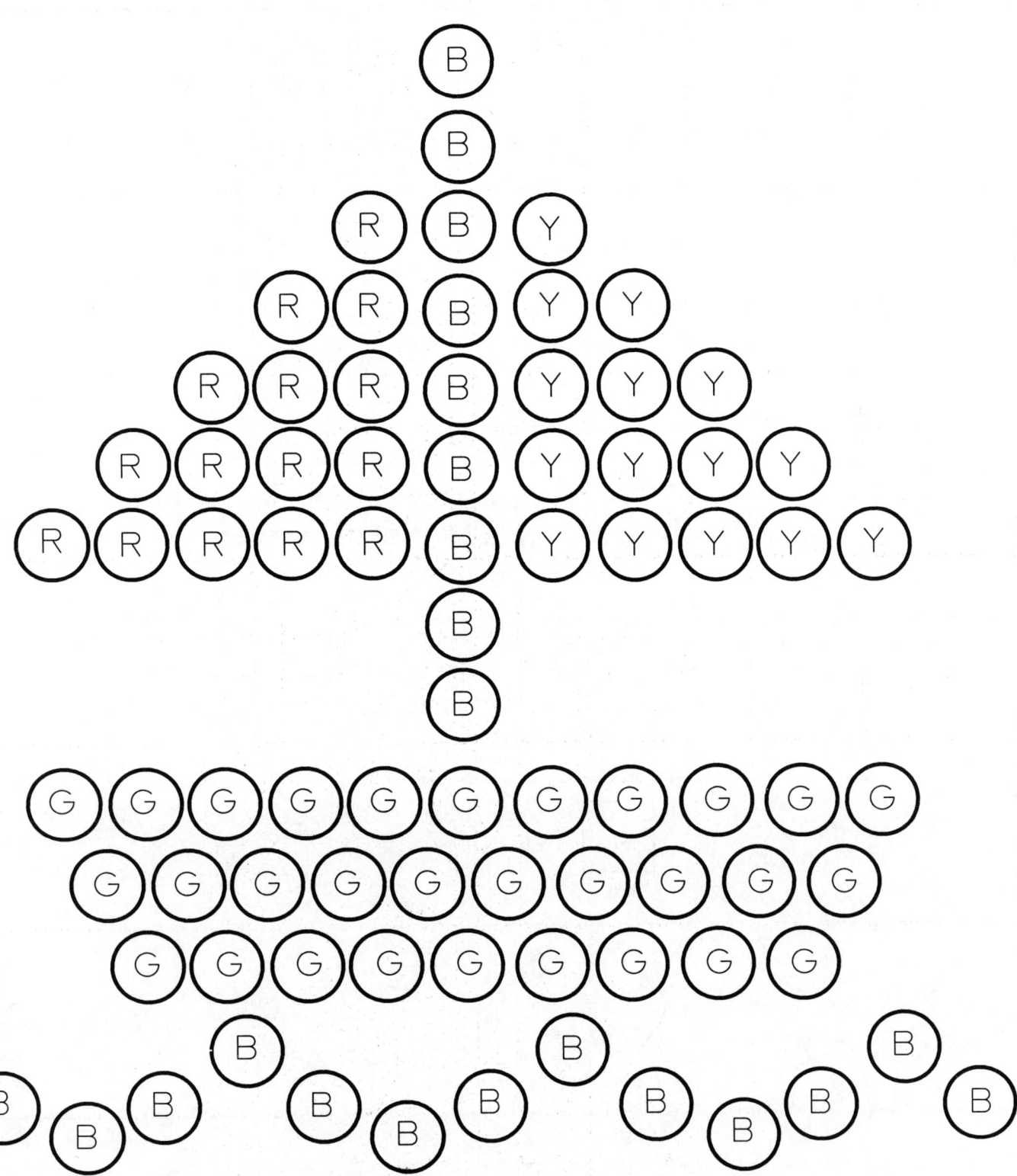

Recycle Sculpture

Objectives

Develop problem-solving and small-motor skills.

Materials Needed

❏ reusable items
❏ tape
❏ construction paper
❏ scissors
❏ glue
❏ crayons
❏ pencil
❏ self-stick labels
❏ project worksheet

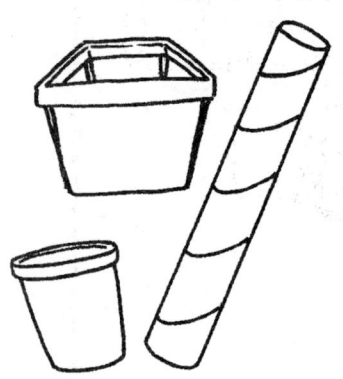

Setting Up the Station

• Invite the children to bring in reusable items, such as cardboard tubes, berry baskets, yogurt containers, egg cartons, plastic-foam trays, and boxes.

• Set out the reusable items, tape, construction paper, scissors, glue, crayons, a pencil, and self-stick labels.

• Copy and display the project worksheet on page 115.

Introducing the Project

Talk with your children about reusing and recycling items we might ordinarily put in the trash. Show them one of the reusable items. Ask them to think of other ways they could use this item instead of just throwing it away. Repeat for some of the other items. Explain to the children the following project steps for reusing those items in their very own sculptures.

The Project

1. Choose four recyclable items, such as a cardboard tube, a yogurt container, a berry basket, and a box.

2. Tape the items together to make a sculpture.

3. Decorate the sculpture with crayon designs and glued-on construction paper scraps.

4. Write your name on a self-stick label and attach it to your sculpture.

Follow-Up

Create an art gallery with the children's Recycle Sculptures. Write each child's name and the name of his or her sculpture on an index card beside it. If you wish, copy the additional worksheets on pages 116 and 117 for the children to complete in class or at home.

Recycle Sculpture

1. Choose 4 items.

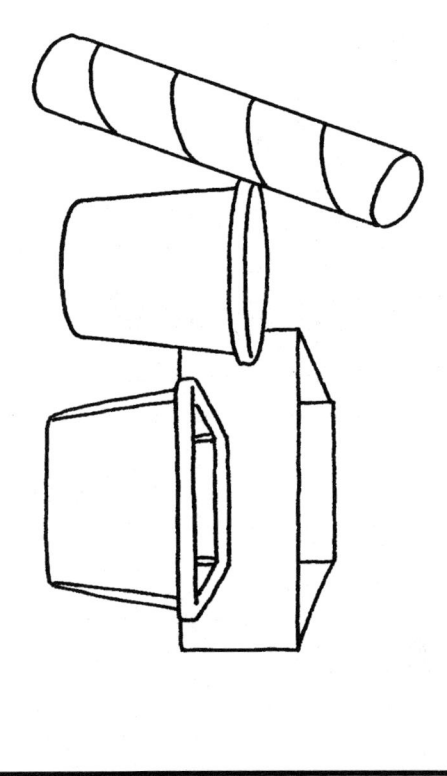

2. Make sculpture. Tape together.

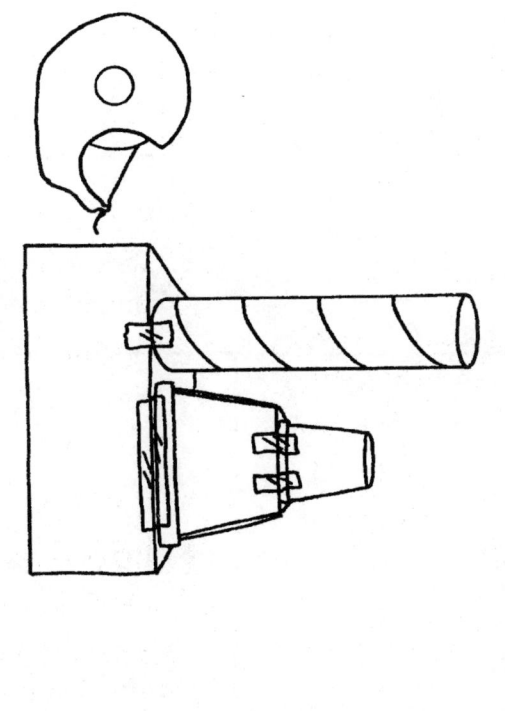

3. Decorate.

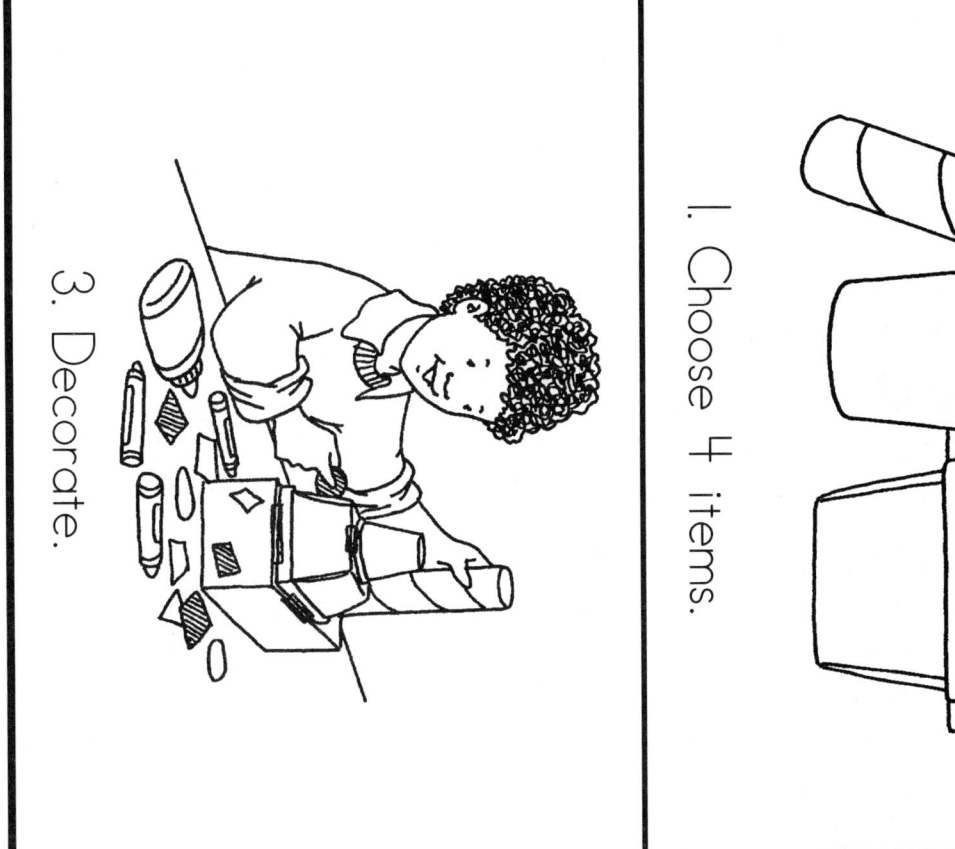

4. Write name on label. Put on sculpture.

Name_____

Draw the rest of the tower.

Name_____

For each box, count the blocks in the sculpture. Write the number on the line.

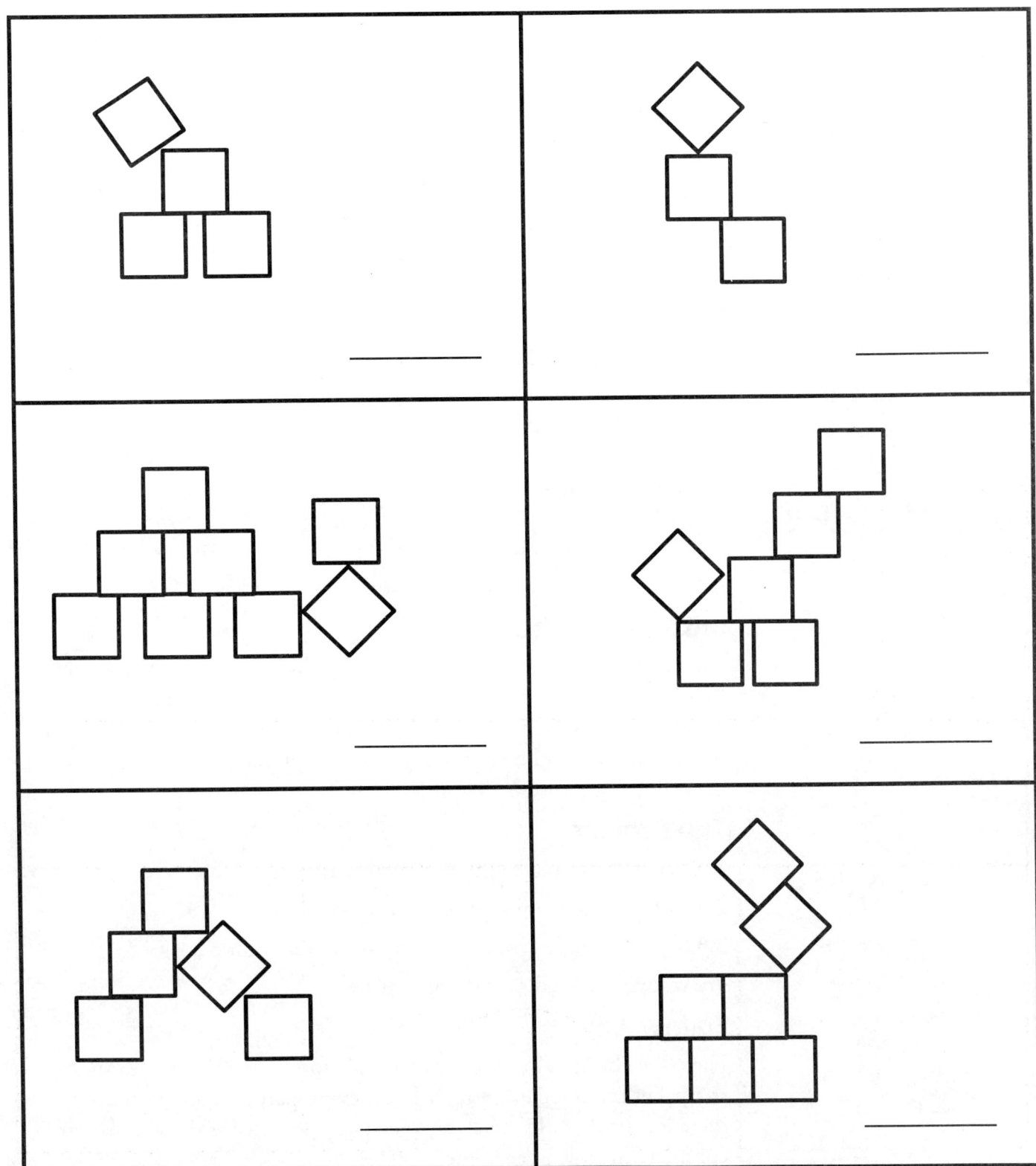

Roll Your Dinner

Objectives

Develop creativity, problem-solving, and small-motor skills.

Materials Needed

❏ food pictures
❏ utensils
❏ air-dry clay
❏ paper plates
❏ pencil
❏ project worksheet

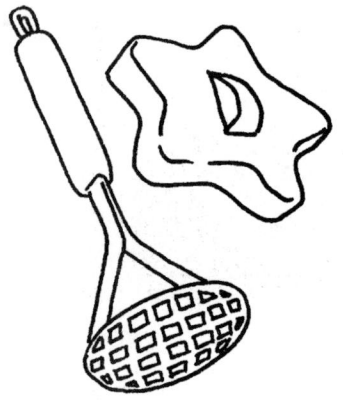

Setting Up the Station

• Hang up pictures of healthy foods.
• Collect utensils that can be used for shaping clay, such as table knives, spoons, cookie cutters, a potato masher, and spatulas.
• Purchase air-dry clay in food colors, such as red, green, yellow, and brown.
• Set out the utensils, clay, paper plates, and a pencil.
• Copy and display the project worksheet on page 119.

Introducing the Project

Ask your children to name their favorite things to eat. What would they prepare if they were making a special meal? Talk about fixing a variety of foods such as vegetables, fruits, grains, and meats. Explain that today they will be preparing a special pretend meal as you go over the following steps for the project.

The Project

1. Select a paper plate and write your name on it.
2. Choose a small amount of each color of clay.
3. Use the utensils to form the clay into pretend food.
4. Arrange the food on the paper plate.

Follow-Up

Have the children bring their plates of "food" to a pretend dinner party. Let them tell everyone what they prepared. If you wish, copy the additional worksheets on pages 120 and 121 for the children to complete in class or at home.

Roll Your Dinner

1. Write name on plate.

2. Choose clay.

3. Make food.

4. Arrange food.

Name_____

Circle the foods you like to eat for dinner.

Name_____

Help the girl find her lunch.

Sack Puppet

Objectives

Practice cutting and gluing skills and develop imagination and creativity.

Materials Needed

❑ paper lunch sacks
❑ pencil
❑ construction paper
❑ scissors
❑ glue
❑ project worksheet

Setting Up the Station

• Set out paper lunch sacks, a pencil, construction paper (scraps are fine), scissors, and glue.
• Make a simple Sack Puppet as a working model.
• Copy and display the project worksheet on page 123.

Introducing the Project

Show your children the Sack Puppet you made. Call attention to how you put your hand in the folds of the puppet and move your fingers to make it "talk." Discuss all the different kinds of things a puppet could be: an animal, a friend, a family member, a story character, etc. Let your puppet explain the following project steps to the children.

The Project

1. Select a paper lunch sack and write your name on it.

2. Cut eye, nose, mouth, and other face shapes out of construction paper.

3. Cut out construction-paper clothes.

4. Glue the face shapes and clothes on the sack to make the puppet.

Follow-Up

Let your children use their puppets to sing songs and put on mini-puppet shows. Encourage the children to name their puppets. If you wish, copy the additional worksheets on pages 124 and 125 for the children to complete in class or at home.

Sack Puppet

1. Write name on sack.

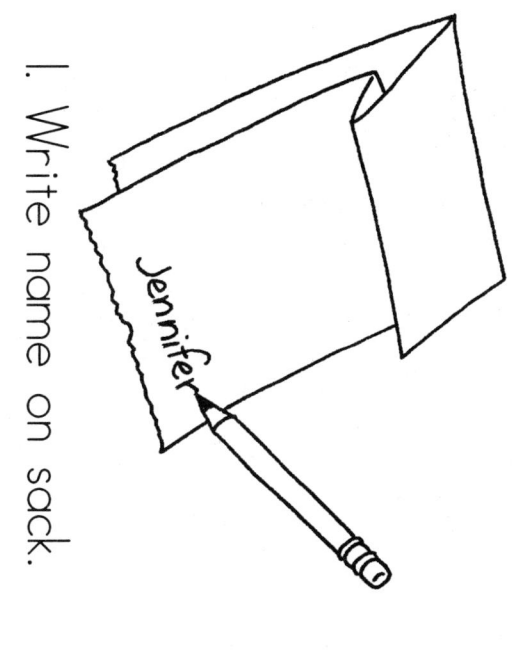

2. Cut out face pieces.

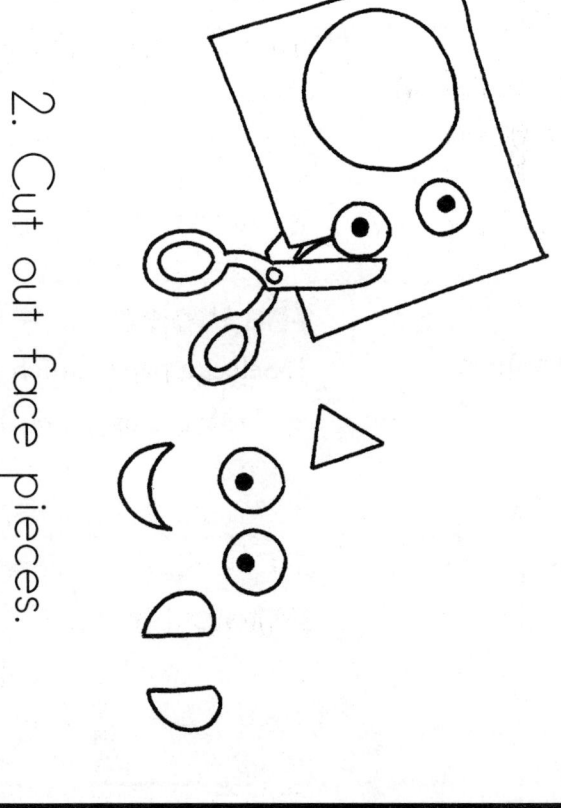

3. Cut out clothes.

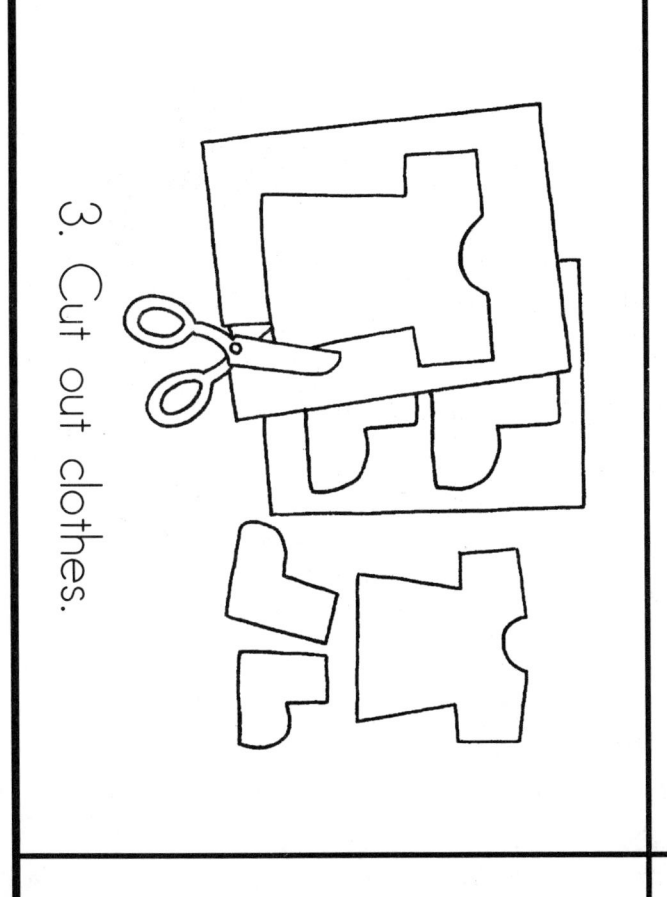

4. Glue face and clothes on sack.

Name_____

In each row, circle the puppet that is different.

Name_____

Color the puppet to match yours.

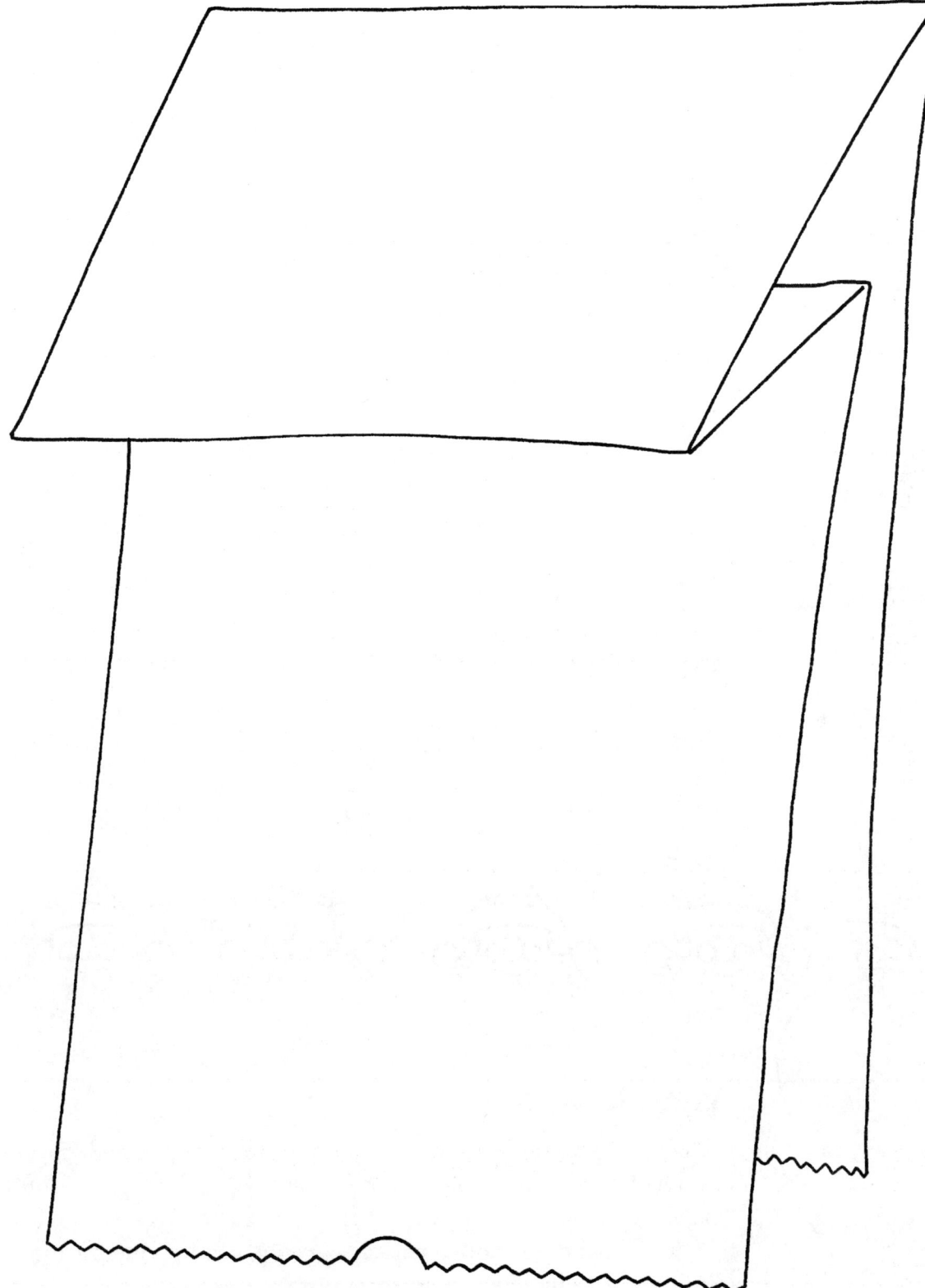

Shape Picture

Objectives

Practice gluing skills and develop imagination and creativity.

Materials Needed

❏ shape pictures
❏ paper shapes
❏ construction paper
❏ pencil
❏ glue
❏ project worksheet

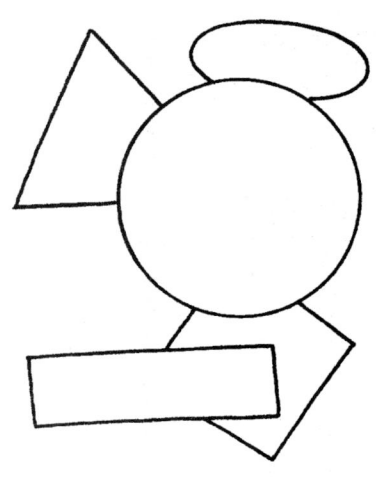

Setting Up the Station

• Find pictures of familiar objects that show different shapes, such as a house with square windows or a car with round wheels.

• Collect circle, triangle, square, and rectangle paper shapes in two sizes. These can be purchased at school supply stores or you can cut your own.

• Set out the paper shapes, construction paper, a pencil, and glue.

• Copy and display the project worksheet on page 127.

Introducing the Project

Show your children the pictures of familiar objects. Have them look for the shapes that make up the object in each picture. Encourage them to look around the room for shapes. Explain the following project steps to them so they can make their own designs from shapes.

The Project

1. Select a sheet of construction paper and write your name on the back.

2. Choose the shapes you would like to work with.

3. Arrange the shapes on the paper until you have the design or object you want.

4. Glue the shapes in place.

Follow-Up

Have the children tell you the names of their creations. Write the name of each child's design on his or her paper. Hang the completed papers on a wall or a bulletin board to make a shape display. If you wish, copy the additional worksheets on pages 128 and 129 for the children to complete in class or at home.

Shape Picture

1. Write name on paper.

Tanya

2. Choose shapes.

3. Arrange shapes.

4. Glue on shapes.

Name_____

Color the picture. △ =red □ =green ○ =blue ▭ =yellow

Name_____

In each row, complete the pattern by drawing the missing shape.

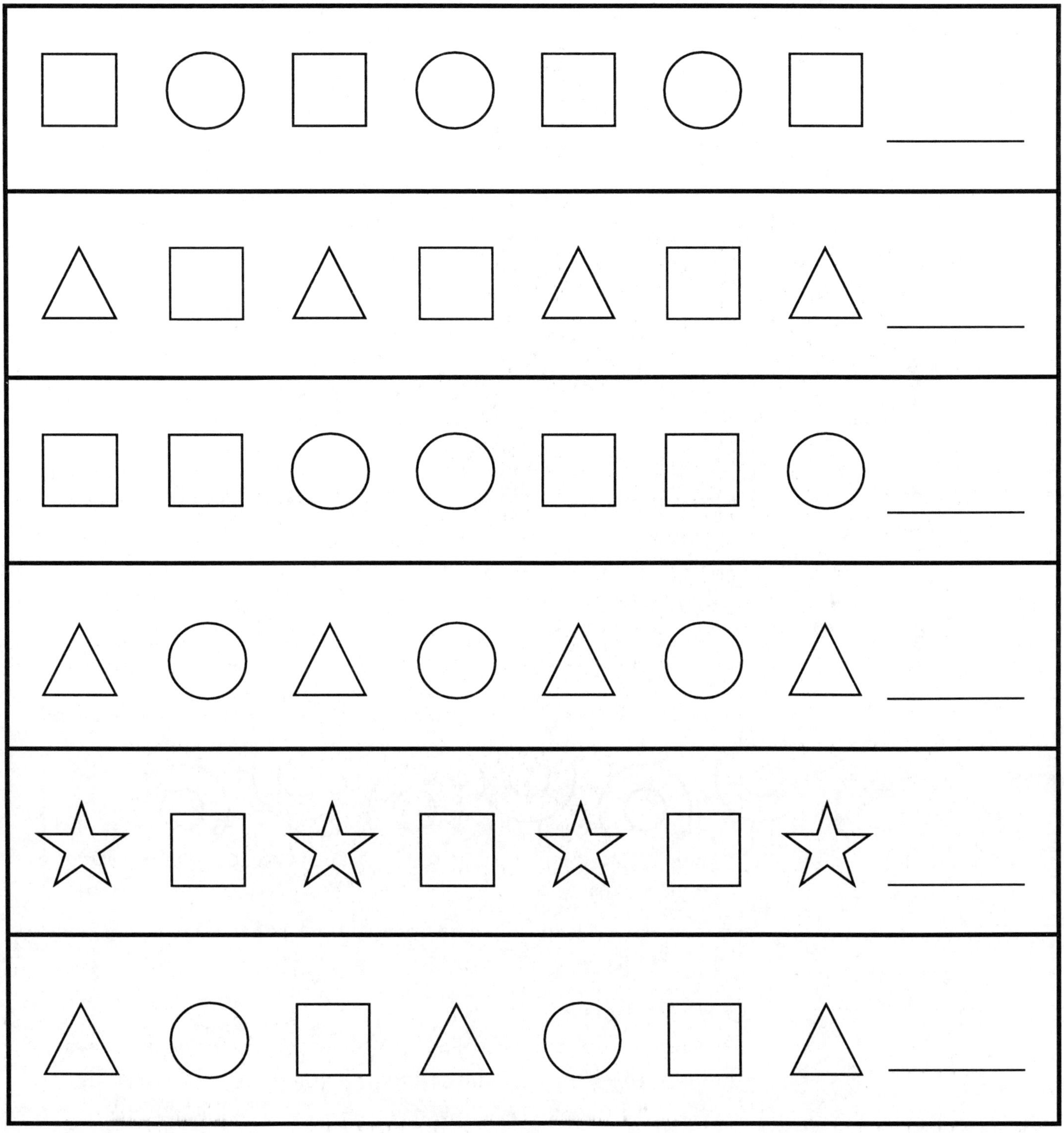

□ ○ □ ○ □ ○ □ ___

△ □ △ □ △ □ △ ___

□ □ ○ ○ □ □ ○ ___

△ ○ △ ○ △ ○ △ ___

☆ □ ☆ □ ☆ □ ☆ ___

△ ○ □ △ ○ □ △ ___

Spaceship

Objectives

Practice cutting and gluing skills and develop creativity.

Materials Needed

- ❑ pictures of spaceships and outer space
- ❑ paper plates
- ❑ pencil
- ❑ scissors
- ❑ glue
- ❑ crayons
- ❑ self-stick stars
- ❑ circle stickers
- ❑ project worksheet

Setting Up the Station

- In the station, hang up pictures of spaceships and outer space.
- Collect two heavy-duty paper plates for each child.
- Set out the paper plates, a pencil, scissors, glue, crayons, self-stick stars, and circle stickers.
- Copy and display the project worksheet on page 131.

Introducing the Project

Discuss rockets and spaceships with your children. Show them the pictures in the station. Ask the children to think about what kind of spaceship they would like to ride in. Explain to them the following project steps for making their own pretend Spaceships for exploring outer space.

The Project

1. Select two paper plates and write your name on the back of one of them.

2. Put glue around the rim of one paper plate.

3. Turn the other plate upside down and place its rim on top of the glue. Hold the plates together and count to 10, to make sure the glue is stuck.

4. Decorate your paper plate Spaceship with crayons and star and circle stickers.

Follow-Up

Display the Spaceships around the room. Read a story about spaceships or space travel to the children. If you wish, copy the additional worksheets on pages 132 and 133 for the children to complete in class or at home.

Spaceship

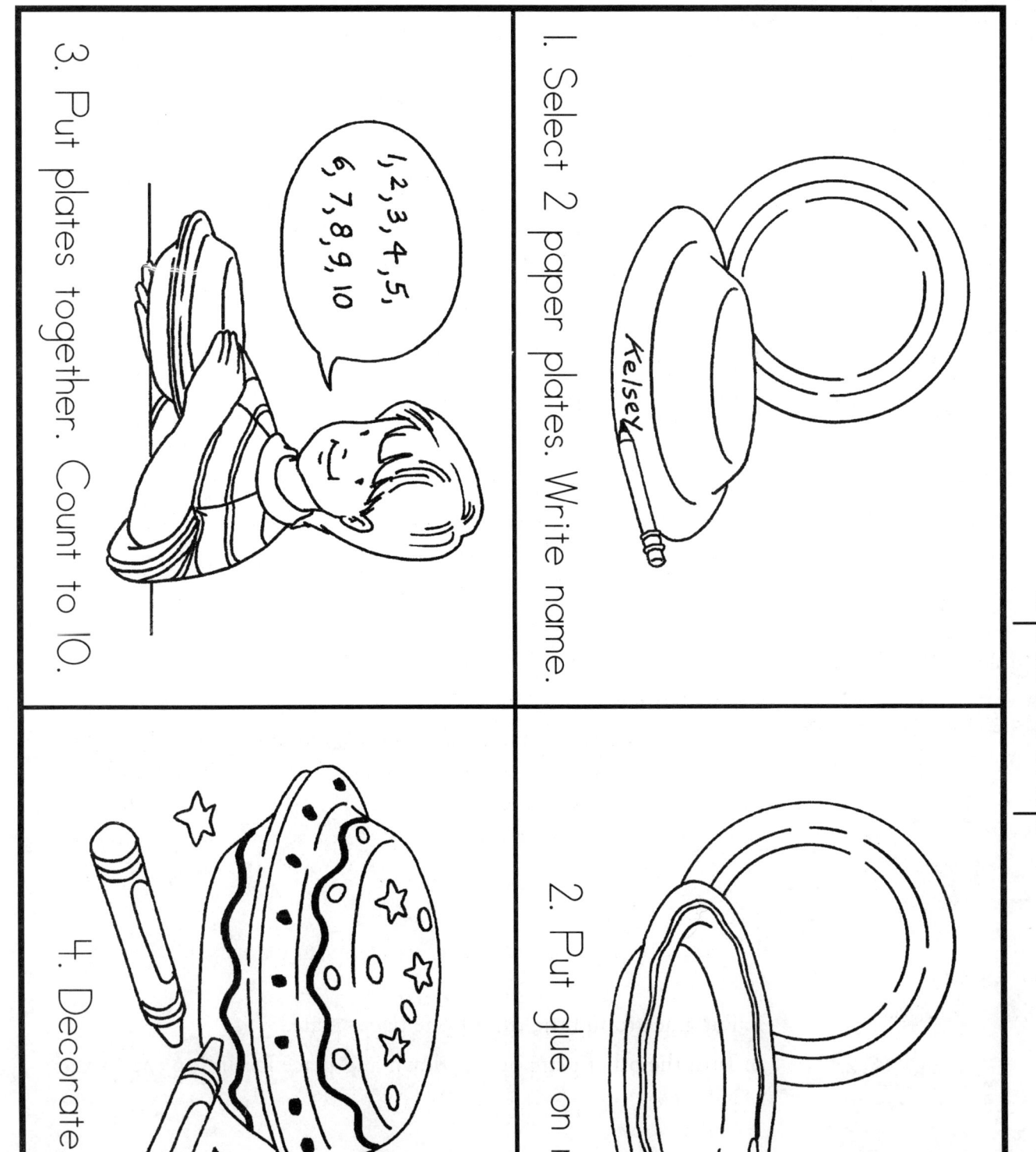

1. Select 2 paper plates. Write name.

2. Put glue on rim.

3. Put plates together. Count to 10.

1, 2, 3, 4, 5,
6, 7, 8, 9, 10

4. Decorate.

Name_____

Count the lights on each spaceship and draw a line to the matching number and word.

 0 zero

 1 one

 3 three

 2 two

 5 five

 4 four

Name_____

Connect the stars to find the Big Dipper.

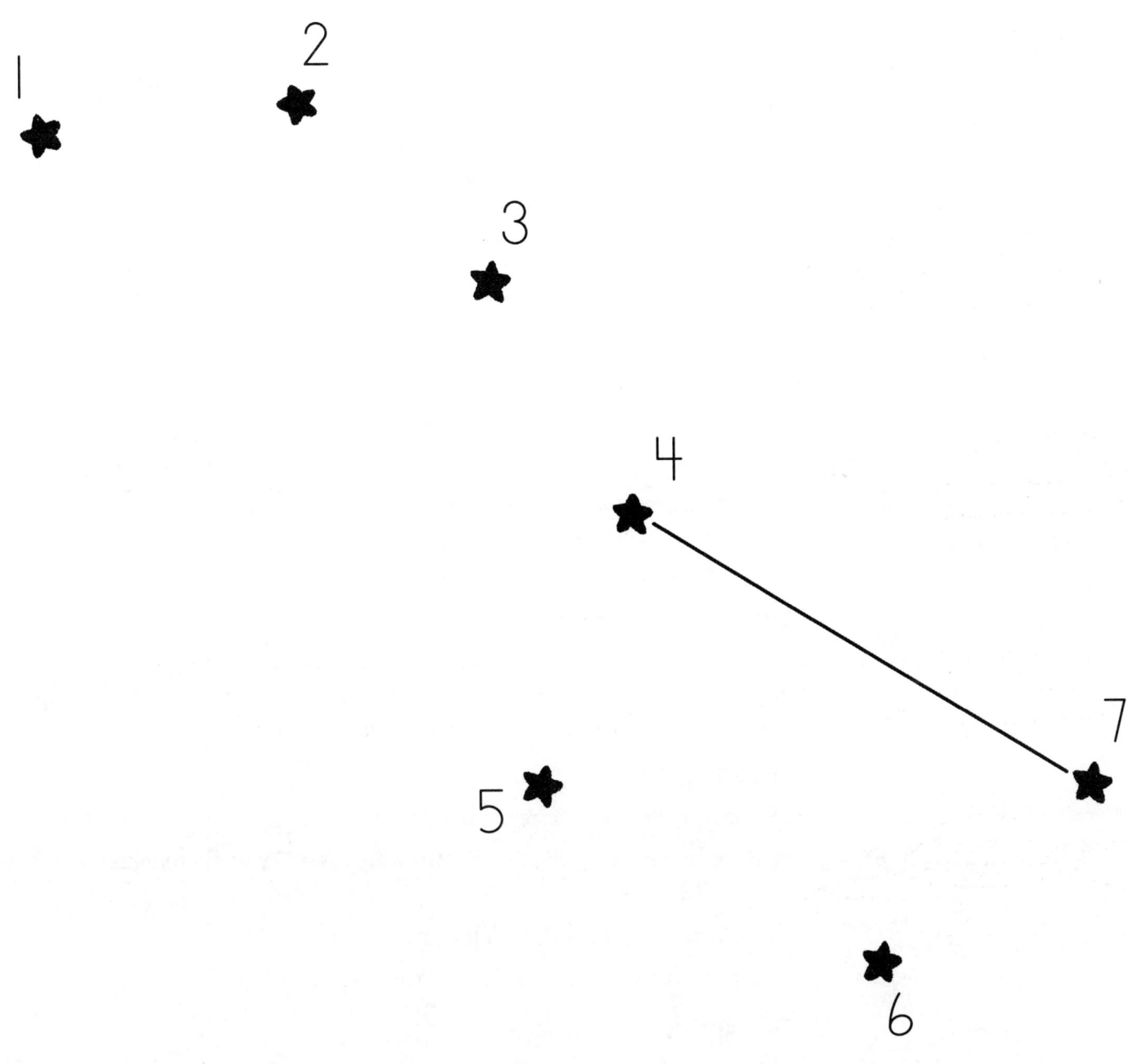

Stick Puppet

Objectives

Practice cutting and gluing skills.

Materials Needed

❑ magazines
❑ scissors
❑ index cards
❑ glue
❑ craft sticks
❑ tape
❑ pencil
❑ project worksheet

Setting Up the Station

- Cut interesting characters (people, animals, cartoon characters, etc.) out of magazines. Make sure each character will fit on an index card.
- Set out the magazine characters, index cards, glue, scissors, craft sticks, tape, and a pencil.
- Copy and display the project worksheet on page 135.

Introducing the Project

Show your children some of the magazine characters you have cut out. Let them think of a name for each one. Explain to them the following project steps for turning the characters into stick puppets.

The Project

1. Select a magazine character that you like and glue it to an index card.
2. Cut off the excess index card, trimming as close to the character as possible.
3. Tape a craft stick to the back of the character.
4. Write your name on the back of the completed puppet.

Follow-Up

Make a simple puppet theater out of a cardboard box. Invite two or three children to bring up their puppets and put on a quick puppet show. Repeat, until everyone has had a turn. If you wish, copy the additional worksheets on pages 136 and 137 for the children to complete in class or at home.

Stick Puppet

1. Select character. Glue to card.

2. Cut around character.

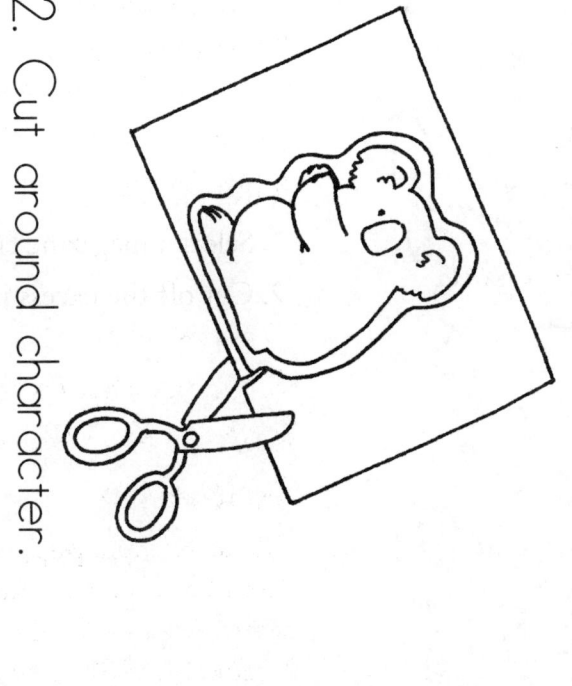

3. Tape craft stick to back.

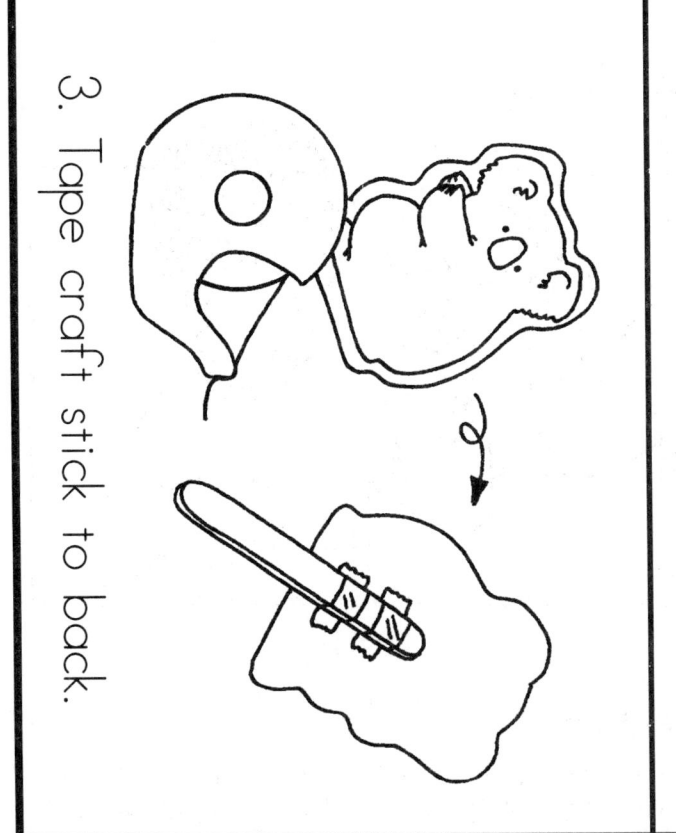

4. Write name on back.

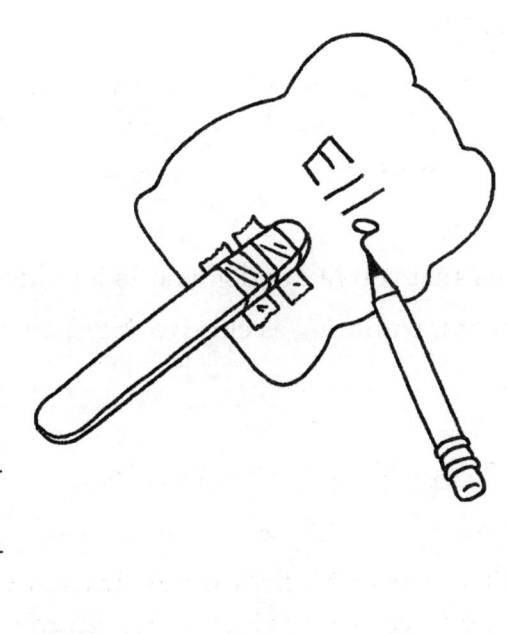

Name_____

Look at each bear's clothes. Draw a line connecting each
bear to where he is going.

Name_____

For each row, circle what happens first.

 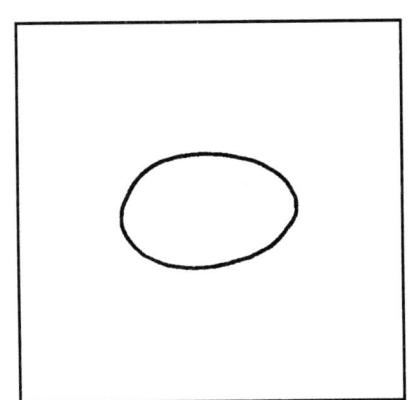 

Tube Trees

Objectives

Develop small-motor skills.

Materials Needed

❑ picture of tree
❑ cardboard tubes
❑ scissors
❑ paper plates
❑ pencil
❑ crayons
❑ project worksheet

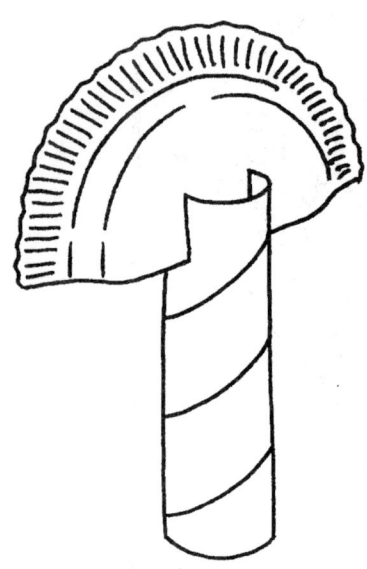

Setting Up the Station

• Display a picture of a deciduous tree in the station.
• Collect a cardboard toilet tissue tube for each child. On the top of each tube, cut two lengthwise slits, about 1 inch long, opposite each other.
• Cut plain white paper plates in half.
• Set out the prepared tubes, paper plate halves, crayons, and a pencil.
• Copy and display the project worksheet on page 139.

Introducing the Project

Show the picture of a tree and discuss the parts of it with your children. Talk about the tree trunk, the branches, and the leaves. Ask the children to name some fruits that grow on trees. Explain to the children the following project steps for making their own fruit trees out of paper plates and cardboard tubes.

The Project

1. Select a paper plate half and write your name on the back.
2. Draw fruit on the front of the paper plate.
3. Color the rest of the paper plate green.
4. Put the plate, straight side down, in the slits of one of the cardboard tubes to make a tree.

Follow-Up

Have the children name the fruits they selected to grow on their trees. Ask them to divide into groups according to the type of fruit. Which fruit has more trees? Are there any unusual fruit trees? If you wish, copy the additional worksheets on pages 140 and 141 for the children to complete in class or at home.

Tube Trees

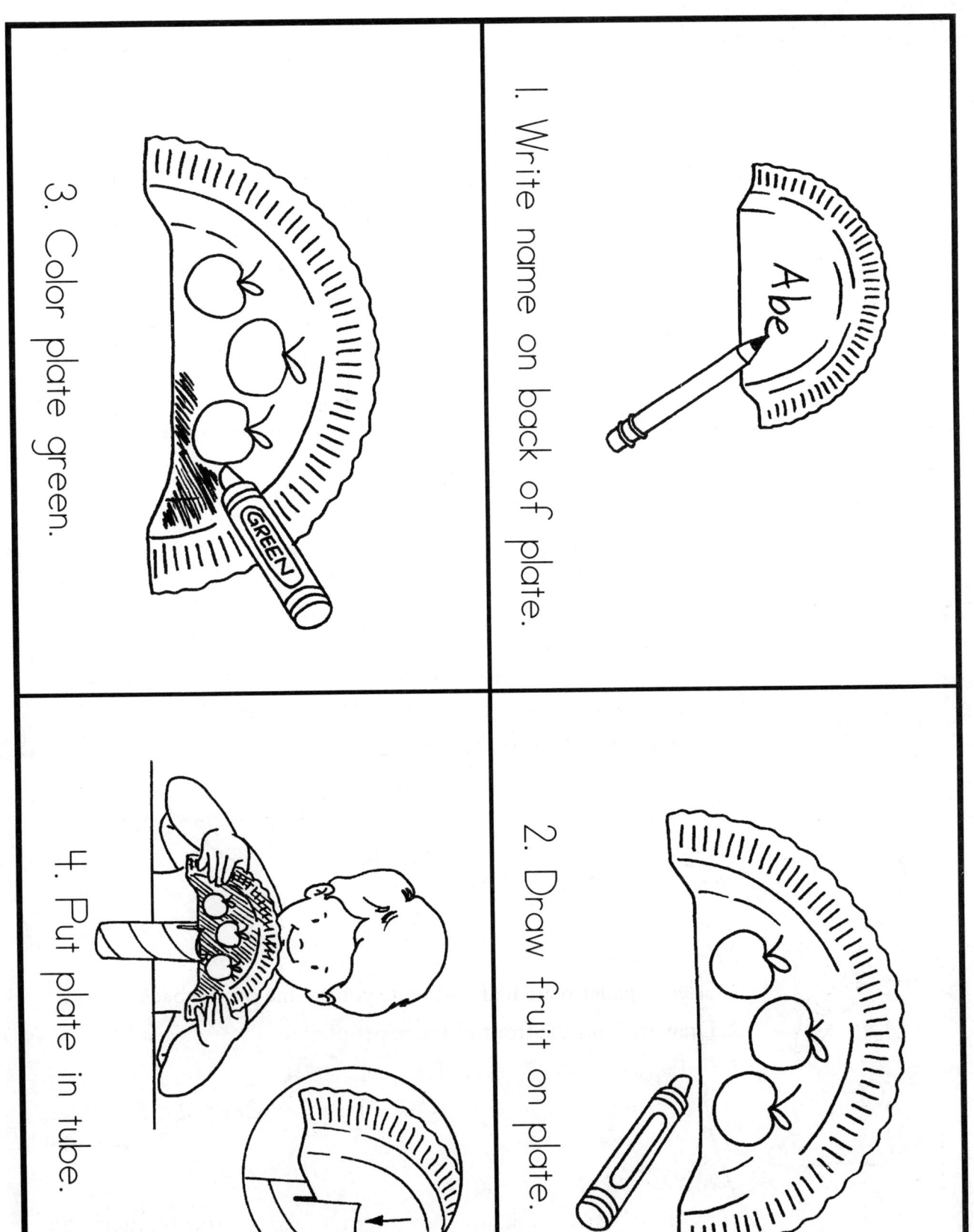

1. Write name on back of plate.

2. Draw fruit on plate.

3. Color plate green.

4. Put plate in tube.

Name_____

Draw more apples to make 10. Color the picture.

Name_____

In each row, add the apples and write the total.

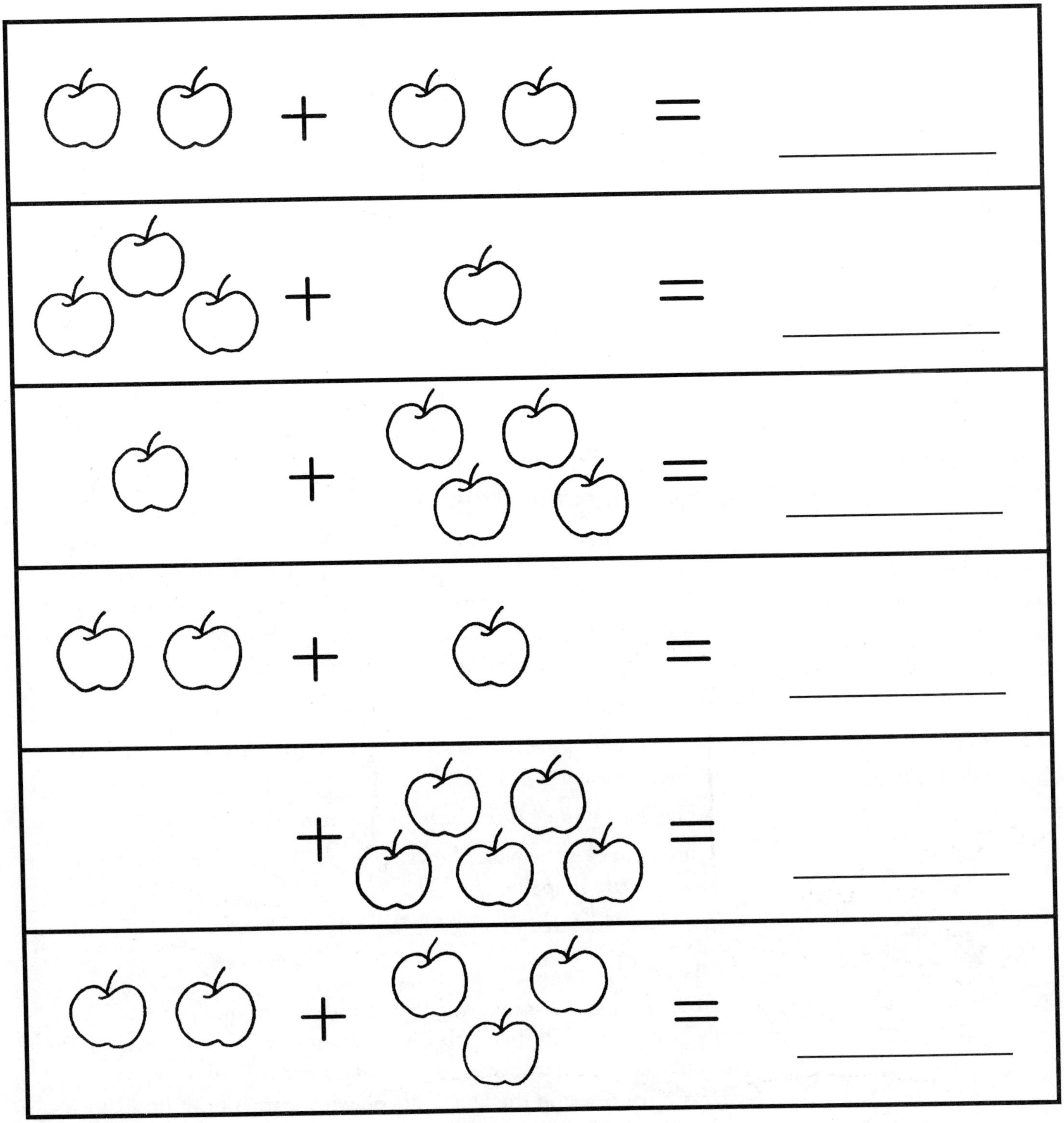

🍎🍎 + 🍎🍎 = _____

🍎🍎🍎 + 🍎 = _____

🍎 + 🍎🍎🍎🍎 = _____

🍎🍎 + 🍎 = _____

+ 🍎🍎🍎🍎🍎 = _____

🍎🍎 + 🍎🍎🍎 = _____

Turtle

Objectives

Practice tracing, cutting, and gluing skills.

Materials Needed

❏ pictures of turtles
❏ turtle pattern worksheet
❏ posterboard
❏ green construction paper
❏ pencil
❏ scissors
❏ paper bowls
❏ glue
❏ crayons
❏ project worksheet

Setting Up the Station

• In the station, hang up pictures of turtles.
• Use the pattern on page 144 to make a turtle pattern out of posterboard for the children to trace around.
• Set out the turtle pattern, green construction paper, a pencil, scissors, paper bowls, glue, and crayons.
• Copy and display the project worksheet on page 143.

Introducing the Project

Show your children the turtle pictures. Ask them to describe the different parts of a turtle. Encourage them to pay special attention to the shell. Is a turtle's shell a particular color? Does it have a pattern on it? What else is unique about a turtle's shell? Explain to them the following project steps for making their own paper turtles.

The Project

1. On a sheet of green construction paper, trace around the turtle pattern and cut it out.

2. Write your name on the back of the turtle shape.

3. Choose one of the paper bowls, put glue on the rim, and glue it to the turtle shape.

4. Decorate the bowl to look like a turtle's shell.

Follow-Up

Let the children hide their turtles around the room. Go for a "turtle walk" to discover all the turtles. Talk about how turtles move. Have the children practice moving slowly like a turtle. Tell or read the story of "The Tortoise and the Hare." If you wish, copy the additional worksheet on page 145 for the children to complete in class or at home.

Turtle

1. Trace around pattern. Cut out.

2. Write name on turtle shape.

3. Glue bowl to turtle shape.

4. Decorate.

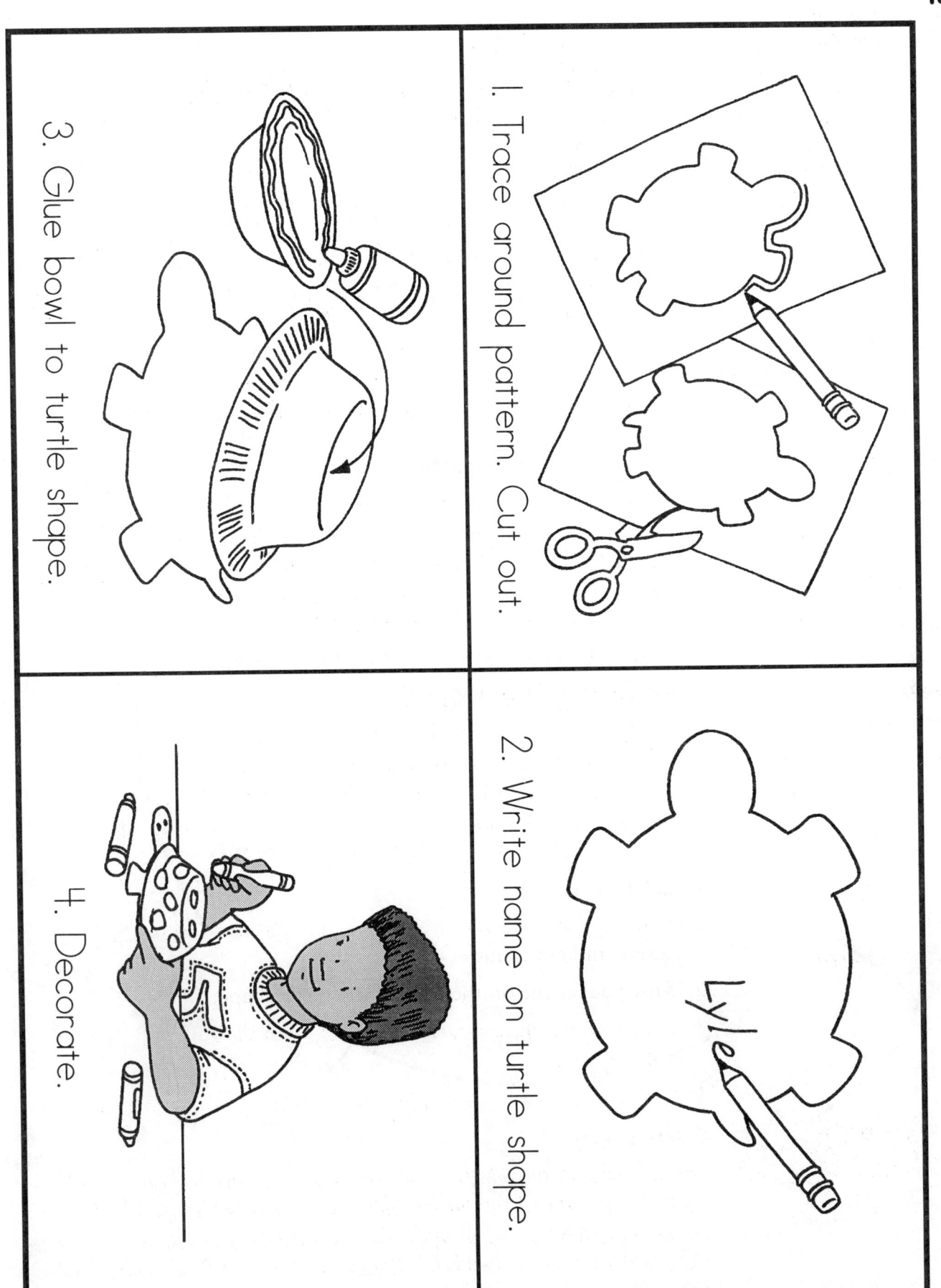

Name_____

Trace each turtle's path to its home.

Weaving

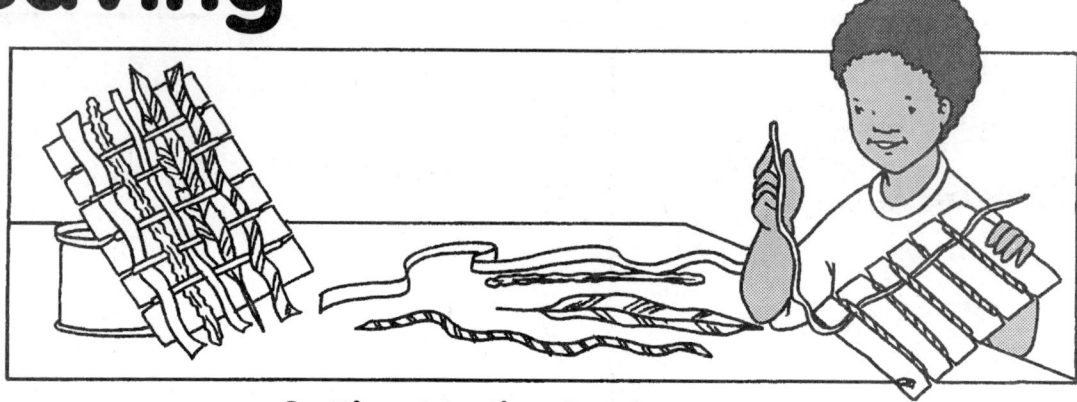

Objectives

Develop problem-solving and small-motor skills.

Materials Needed

- ❏ woven handicrafts
- ❏ cardboard
- ❏ ruler
- ❏ scissors
- ❏ felt tip marker
- ❏ hole punch
- ❏ yarn
- ❏ pencil
- ❏ weaving materials
- ❏ project worksheet

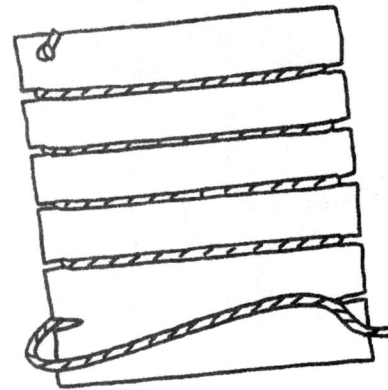

Setting Up the Station

- Collect a few woven items to display in the station.
- Cut cardboard into 7-by-5-inch rectangles. (Old cereal boxes and gift boxes work especially well for this.) Cut one rectangle for each child, plus one for yourself.
- To turn the cardboard rectangles into weaving boards, draw five 1-inch-long lines on each long side.
- Cut thick yarn into 48-inch lengths.
- Collect a variety of weaving materials, such as craft feathers, ribbon, fabric strips, pipe cleaners, felt strips, and twigs.
- Set out the prepared weaving boards, yarn, a pencil, scissors, and weaving materials.
- Copy and display the project worksheet on page 147.

Introducing the Project

Show your children the woven handicraft items. Point out the various patterns and how the yarn, or whatever material was used, goes over and under, over and under. Show them your weaving board. Explain and demonstrate the following project steps to the children.

The Project

1. Select one of the weaving boards and write your name on the back.
2. Cut along each of the lines drawn on the board to make slits.
3. Hold the yarn on the back of the weaving board and wind it around the board, pulling it into each slit. Make sure the yarn is pulled snugly each time.
4. Select six items and weave them over and under the yarn.

Follow-Up

Hang up the children's weavings. Ask them to notice ways that their weavings are the same and ways that they are different. If you wish, copy the additional worksheets on pages 148 and 149 for the children to complete in class or at home.

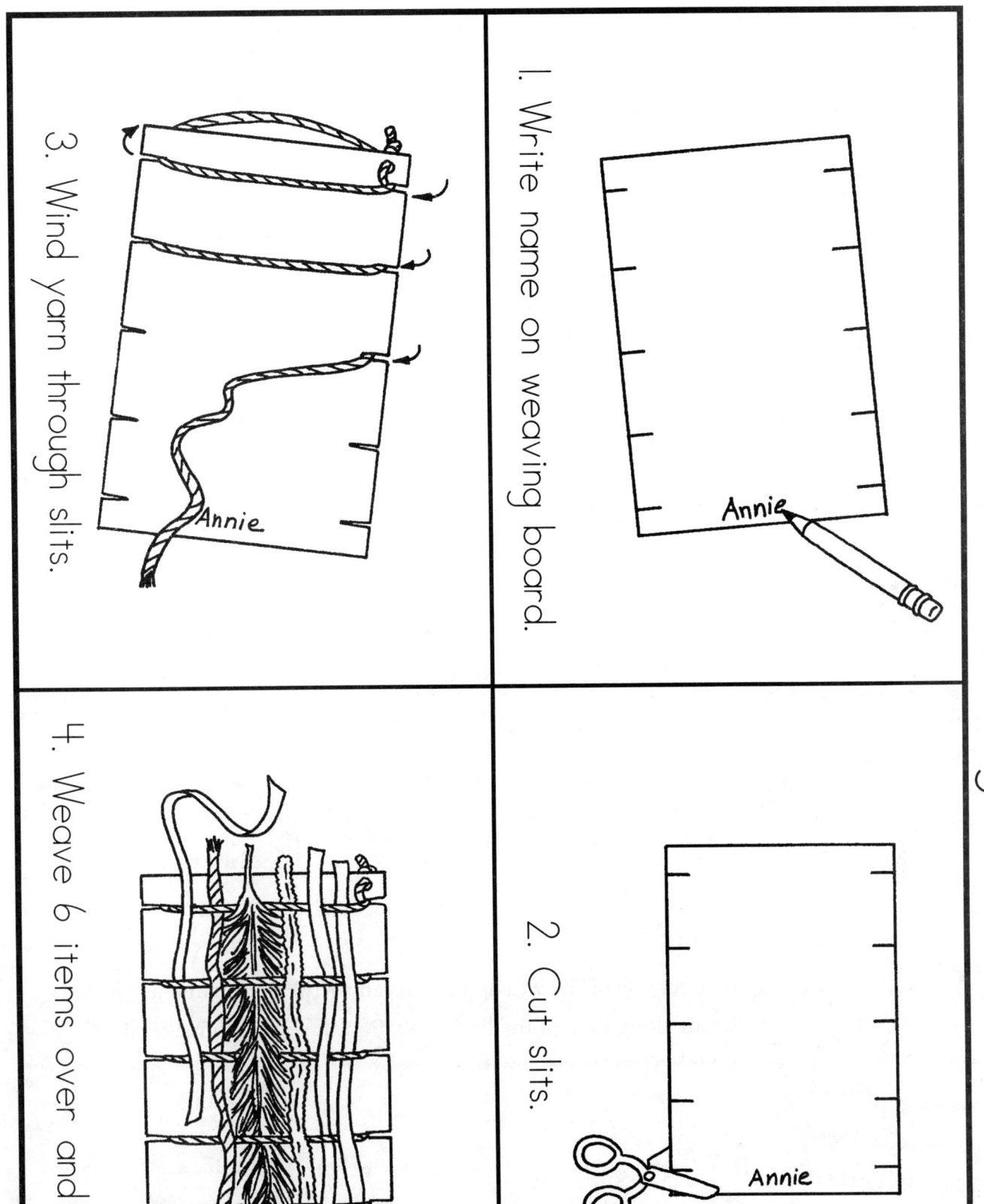

1. Write name on weaving board.

2. Cut slits.

3. Wind yarn through slits.

4. Weave 6 items over and under.

Weaving

Name_____

In each box, circle the bear that is over.

In each box, circle the bear that is under.

Name_____

Color the stripes on the rug to make a pattern.

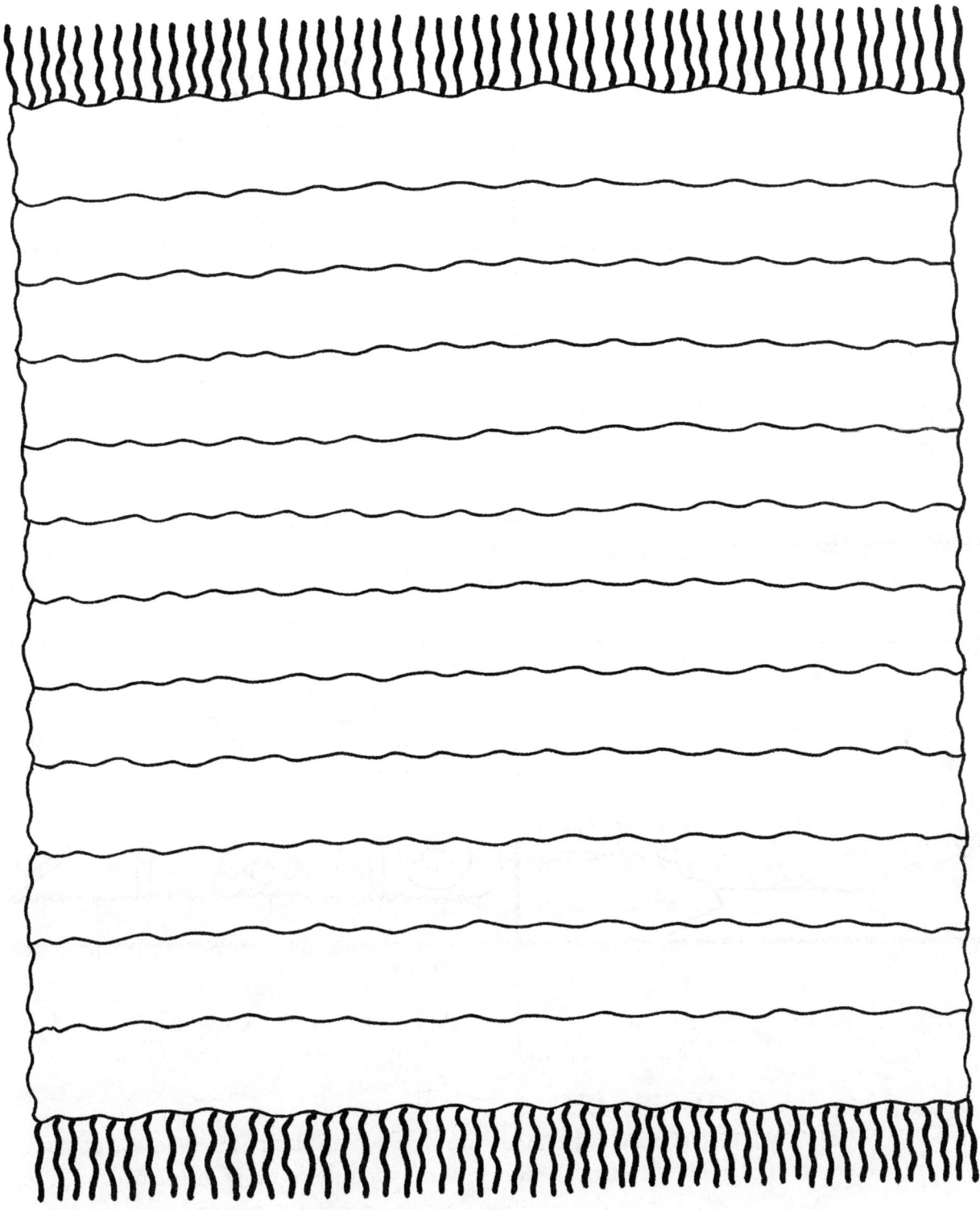

Windsock

Objectives

Develop creativity and problem-solving skills.

Materials Needed

❑ real windsock and kite
❑ crepe paper
❑ ruler
❑ scissors
❑ construction paper
❑ pencil
❑ crayons
❑ rubber stamps
❑ ink pads
❑ tape
❑ project worksheet
❑ yarn

Setting Up the Station

• In the station, hang up a real windsock and kite.
• Cut crepe paper into 2-foot-long streamers, making six for each child.
• Collect various colors of 12-by-18-inch construction paper.
• Set out the crepe paper streamers, construction paper, a pencil, crayons, rubber stamps, ink pads, and tape.
• Copy and display the project worksheet on page 151.

Introducing the Project

Point out the windsock and kite to your children. What happens to windsocks and kites in the wind? Explain to the children the following steps for making their own Windsocks.

The Project

1. Select a sheet of construction paper and write your name on the back.

2. Decorate the paper with crayons and rubber stamp designs.

3. On the back side of the paper, tape six streamers to the long bottom edge.

4. Roll the paper into a cylinder, with the decorated side out. Tape the edges together.

Follow-Up

Help the children add yarn hangers to their Windsocks. Let them take their Windsocks outside and watch them blow in the breeze. If you wish, copy the additional worksheets on pages 152 and 153 for the children to complete in class or at home.

1. Write name on paper.

2. Decorate paper.

3. Tape 6 streamers to the back.

4. Roll paper. Tape.

Windsock

Name_____

Color the windsock to match yours.

Name_____

Circle each object that is blowing in the wind.

Yarn Art

Objectives

Develop creativity and small-motor skills.

Materials Needed

❑ yarn
❑ scissors
❑ glue
❑ bowl
❑ construction paper
❑ pencil
❑ project worksheet

Setting Up the Station

• Cut several different colors of yarn into lengths ranging from 2 to 12 inches.

• Pour a small of amount of glue into a bowl.

• Set out the yarn pieces, the bowl of glue, construction paper, and a pencil.

• Copy and display the project worksheet on page 155.

Introducing the Project

Talk about lines with your children. On a sheet of construction paper, draw different kinds of lines for them, including straight lines, curvy lines, zigzag lines, lines curved into circles, and so on. Tell the children they will have an opportunity to make line designs with yarn and explain the following project steps. You may wish to demonstrate the second step of dipping yarn into the bowl of glue and squeezing off the excess glue.

The Project

1. Select a sheet of construction paper and write your name on the back of it.

2. Choose a piece of yarn, dip it in the bowl of glue, and squeeze off the excess glue.

3. Arrange the gluey yarn piece on the construction paper.

4. Repeat with other pieces of yarn to create your design.

Follow-Up

Display the children's Yarn Art on a wall or a bulletin board. Ask them to notice all the different colors and designs that were used to create the art. If you wish, copy the additional worksheets on pages 156 and 157 for the children to complete in class or at home.

Yarn Art

1. Write name on paper.

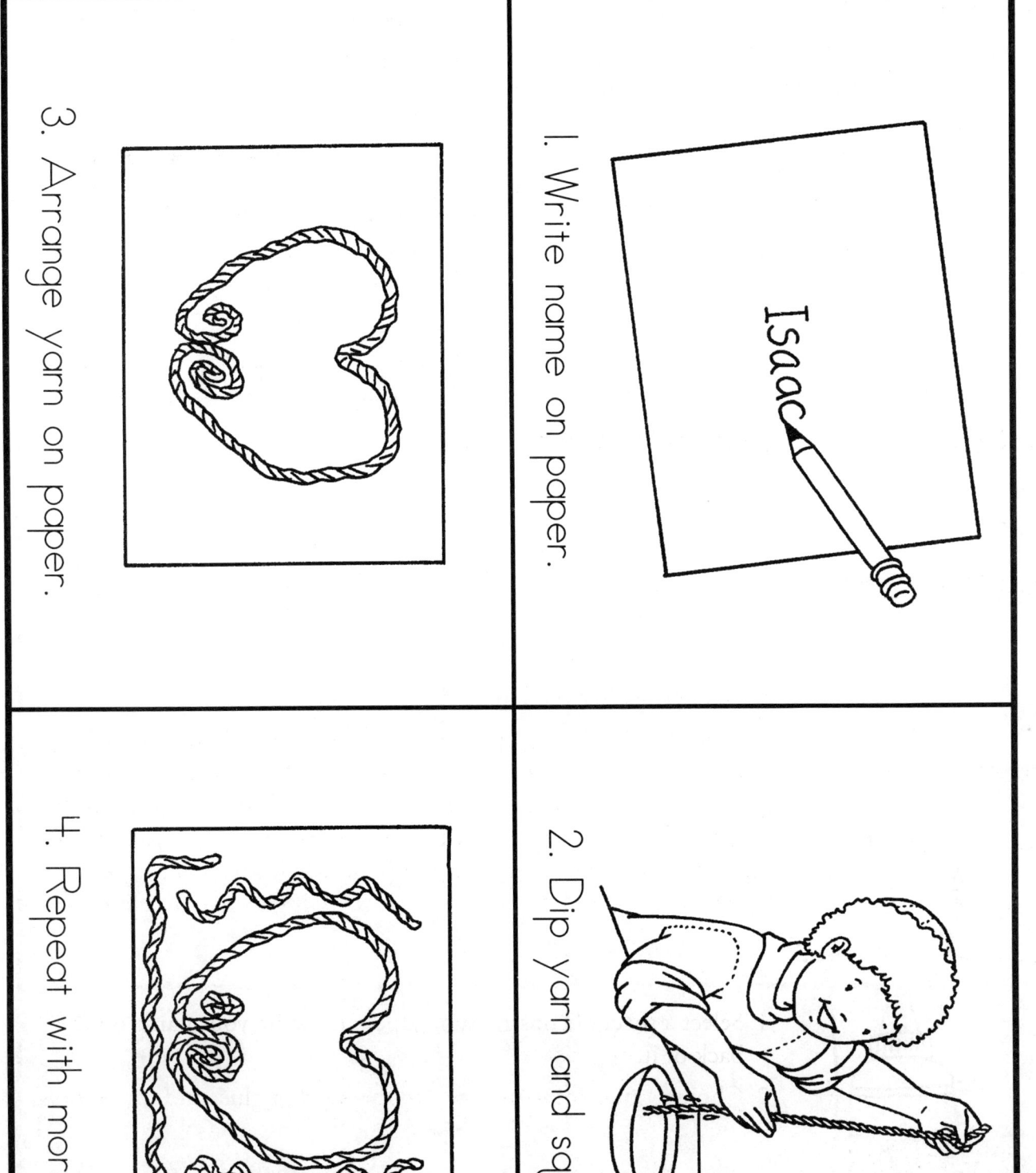

2. Dip yarn and squeeze.

3. Arrange yarn on paper.

4. Repeat with more yarn.

Name_____

In each box, draw one more of that shape.

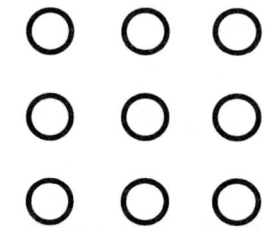

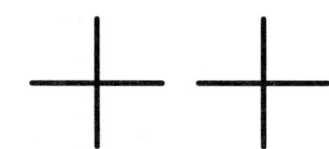

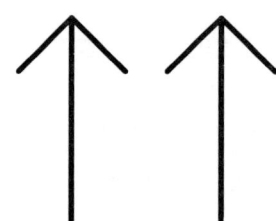

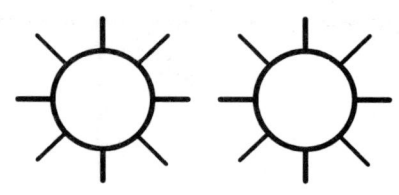

Name_____

In each box, circle the longest object.

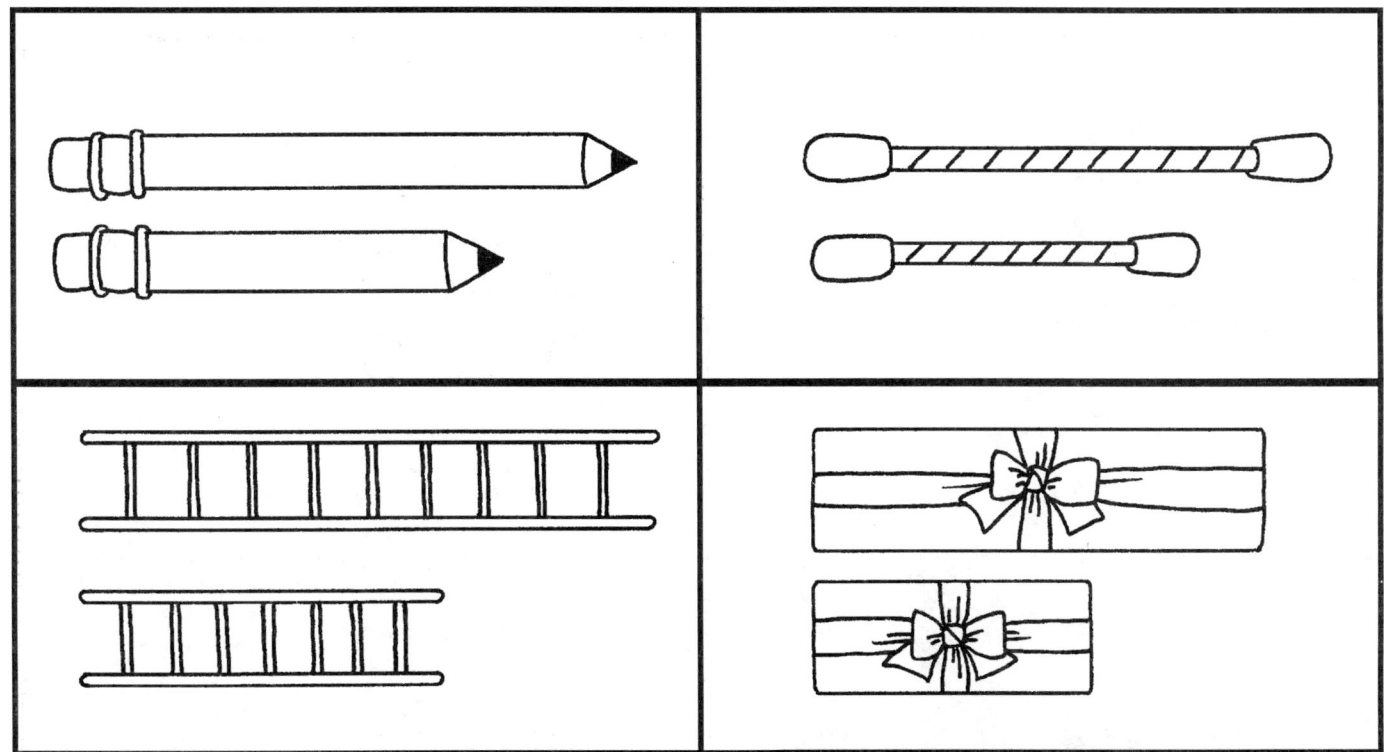

In each box, circle the shortest object.

Teacher Resources
from Totline® Publications

Celebrations

Easy, practical ideas for celebrating holidays and special days around the world. Plus ideas for making ordinary days special.

**Celebrating
Likes and Differences**
Small World Celebrations
Special Day Celebrations
Great Big Holiday Celebrations

Theme-A-Saurus®

Classroom-tested, around-the-curriculum activities organized into imaginative units. Great for implementing a child-directed program.

**Multisensory
Theme-A-Saurus**
Theme-A-Saurus
Theme-A-Saurus II
Toddler Theme-A-Saurus
Alphabet Theme-A-Saurus
**Nursery Rhyme
Theme-A-Saurus**
Storytime Theme-A-Saurus

1•2•3 Series

Open-ended, age-appropriate, cooperative, and no-lose experiences for working with preschool children.

1•2•3 Art
1•2•3 Games
1•2•3 Colors
1•2•3 Puppets
1•2•3 Reading & Writing
**1•2•3 Rhymes,
Stories & Songs**
1•2•3 Math
1•2•3 Science
1•2•3 Shapes

Snacks Series

Easy, educational recipes for healthy eating and expanded learning.

Super Snacks
Healthy Snacks
Teaching Snacks
Multicultural Snacks

Piggyback® Songs

New songs sung to the tunes of childhood favorites. No music to read! Easy for adults and children to learn. Chorded for guitar or autoharp.

Piggyback Songs
More Piggyback Songs
**Piggyback Songs
for Infants & Toddlers**
**Piggyback Songs
in Praise of God**
**Piggyback Songs
in Praise of Jesus**
Holiday Piggyback Songs
Animal Piggyback Songs
Piggyback Songs for School
Piggyback Songs to Sign
Spanish Piggyback Songs
**More Piggyback Songs
for School**

Busy Bees

These seasonal books help two- and three-year-olds discover the world around them through their senses. Each book includes fun activity and learning ideas, songs, snack ideas, and more!

Busy Bees—SPRING
Busy Bees—SUMMER
Busy Bees—FALL
Busy Bees—WINTER

101 Tips for Directors

Great ideas for managing a preschool or daycare. These hassle-free, handy hints are a great help.

Staff and Parent Self-Esteem
Parent Communication
Health and Safety
Marketing Your Center
**Resources for You
and Your Center**
Child Development Training

101 Tips for Toddler Teachers

Designed for adults who work with toddlers.

Classroom Management
Discovery Play
Dramatic Play
Large Motor Play
Small Motor Play
Word Play

101 Tips for Preschool Teachers

Valuable, fresh ideas for adults who work with young children.

Creating Theme Environments
Encouraging Creativity
Developing Motor Skills
Developing Language Skills
Teaching Basic Concepts
Spicing Up Learning Centers

Problem Solving Safari

This unique series teaches teachers to help children problem-solve and think for themselves. Each book includes scenarios from children's real play and possible solutions.

Problem Solving Safari—Art
Problem Solving Safari—Blocks
**Problem Solving Safari—
Dramatic Play**
**Problem Solving Safari—
Manipulatives**
**Problem Solving Safari—
Outdoors**
**Problem Solving Safari—
Science**

The Best of Totline® Series

Collections of some of the finest, most useful material published in *Totline Magazine* over the years.

The Best of Totline
**The Best of Totline
Parent Flyers**

Early Learning at its Best

For parents and children: books, posters, puzzles and more from Totline® Publications

A Year of Fun

Age-specific books detailing how young children grow and change and what parents can do to lay a strong foundation for later learning.

Just for Babies
Just for Ones
Just for Twos
Just for Threes
Just for Fours
Just for Fives

Getting Ready for School

Fun, easy-to-follow ideas for developing essential skills that preschoolers need before they can successfully achieve higher levels of learning.

Ready to Learn Colors, Shapes, and Numbers
Ready to Write and Develop Motor Skills
Ready to Read
Ready to Communicate
Ready to Listen and Explore the Senses

Learning Everywhere

Teaches parents to become aware of the everyday opportunities for teaching their children about language, art, science, math, problem solving, self-esteem, and more!

Teaching House
Teaching Town
Teaching Trips

Beginning Fun With Art

Introduce young children to the fun of art while developing coordination skills and building self-confidence.

Craft Sticks • Crayons • Felt
Glue • Paint • Paper Shapes
Modeling Dough • Yarn
Tissue Paper • Scissors
Rubber Stamps • Stickers

Beginning Fun With Science

Make science fun with these quick, safe, easy-to-do activities that lead to discovery and spark the imagination.

Bugs & Butterflies
Plants & Flowers
Magnets
Rainbows & Colors
Sand & Shells
Water & Bubbles

Teaching Tales

Each of these children's books includes a delightful story plus related activity ideas that expand on the story's theme.

Kids Celebrate the Alphabet
Kids Celebrate Numbers
Ellie the Evergreen
The Wishing Fish
The Bear and the Mountain
Huff and Puff's Snowy Day
Huff and Puff on Groundhog Day
Huff and Puff's Hawaiian Rainbow
Huff and Puff Go to Camp
Huff and Puff on Fourth of July
Huff and Puff Around the World
Huff and Puff Go to School
Huff and Puff on Halloween
Huff and Puff on Thanksgiving
Huff and Puff's Foggy Christmas

Learning Puzzles

Designed to challenge as children grow. Each giant floor puzzle offers learning opportunities, plus teaches basic matching and thinking skills.

Kids Celebrate Numbers Beginning Floor Puzzle
Kids Celebrate the Alphabet Beginning Floor Puzzle
Bear Hugs 4-in-1 Puzzle Set
Busy Bees 4-in-1 Puzzle Set

Two-Sided Circle Puzzles

Double-sided, giant floor puzzles designed in a circle with cutout pieces for extra learning and fun.

Underwater Adventure
African Adventure

Work and Play Together Posters

A colorful collection of cuddly bear posters showing adult and children bears playing and working together. Each 17"x 22".

We Build Together
We Cook Together
We Play Together
We Read Together
We Sing Together
We Work Together

Bear Hugs® Sing-Along Health Posters

Encourage young children to develop good health habits with these posters. Additional learning activities on back!

We Brush Our Teeth
We Can Exercise
We Cover our Coughs and Sneezes
We Eat Good Food
We Get Our Rest
We Wash Our Hands

If you like Totline® Books, you'll love Totline® Magazine!

For fresh ideas that challenge and engage young children in active learning, reach for **Totline Magazine**—Proven ideas from innovative teachers!

Each issue includes

- Seasonal learning themes
- Stories, songs, and rhymes
- Open-ended art projects
- Science explorations
- Reproducible parent pages
- Ready-made teaching materials
- Activities just for toddlers
- Reproducible healthy snack recipes
- Special pull-outs

Receive a free copy of Totline® Magazine by calling 800-609-1724 for subscription information.